李小龍
截拳道秘密

揭開

李小龍之謎

BRUCE LEE

The Tao of the Dragon Warrior

Louis Chunovic

in cooperation with the Bruce Lee Estate

ST. MARTIN'S GRIFFIN

New York

My thanks to Linda Lee Cadwell,
a remarkable woman, for her hospitality, diligence, and trust.
The photographs collected here, many never before seen publicly,
are from her archive.

For my nephews, Brian and Jesse

Bruce and Linda with Shannon looking on.

BRUCE LEE: The Tao of the Dragon Warrior.
Copyright © 1996 by MCA Publishing Rights, a Division of MCA Inc.
All rights reserved. Printed in the United States of America. No part of this book
may be used or reproduced in any manner whatsoever without
written permission except in the case of brief quotations embodied in
critical articles or reviews. For information, address St. Martin's Press,
175 Fifth Avenue, New York, N.Y. 10010.

Design by Michael Mendelsohn at MM Design 2000, Inc.

Library of Congress Cataloging-in-Publication Data

Chunovic, Louis.
  Bruce Lee: the tao of the dragon warrior / by Louis Chunovic in
cooperation with the Bruce Lee estate. —1st St. Martin's Griffin ed.
      p.   cm.
  ISBN 0–312–14290–0
  1. Lee, Bruce, 1940–1973.   2. Actors—United States—Biography.
3. Martial artists—United States—Biography.   I. Title
PN2287.L2897C49   1996
791.43′028′092—dc20
  [B]   96–6154

10   9   8   7   6   5   4   3

Table of Contents

Bruce, Linda, and Brandon during the *Green Hornet* days in Los Angeles.

Preface

It has been well documented that Bruce suffered through difficult times while climbing the ladder to success. However, the significance of these hard times and how they motivated Bruce to "walk on" deserve further exploration. It is from these lessons that we can discover just what made Bruce a unique individual.

Bruce was an accomplished martial artist, a fitness devotee, and a gifted actor. His greatest contribution, however, lies in a field that is rarely discussed. Bruce Lee was without a doubt the most self-motivated man I have ever known. Once Bruce decided he was going to achieve something, there was no question that it would happen. This process of decision making was not lightly undertaken—in fact it was often a grueling process of introspection, of ranking priorities, of delayed gratification, of trying and failing, of redirecting goals and learning, always learning, from these experiences.

Bruce had a concrete symbol of his struggle that he kept with him during these early years. That symbol was simply his pair of glasses. Extremely nearsighted, Bruce wore contact lenses in public but often wore his Coke-bottle glasses at home. Like most of us with severe vision deficiency, Bruce sometimes fell asleep with his glasses on, or he wore them while working out, when they might go flying across the room from the force of his exertion. The point is that this became an abused pair of spectacles, and during those years Bruce could not afford to buy a new pair. These glasses underwent ingenious repairs—the earpieces were wired on, the frames around the lenses were taped and retaped. This was a pair of glasses that only a mother could love.

To Bruce this was not just a pair of sad-looking glasses.

This was a tool of self-motivation. In the last two years of his life, when we lived in Hong Kong and Bruce was achieving his dreams and could afford several pairs of glasses, he always kept the orphan pair on his desk as a reminder of a stage in his life he did not want to repeat. Picking up those spectacles and swinging them from a broken earpiece, he would tell me that never again would he be in the position where he could not afford even such a bare necessity as a pair of glasses. And when he said it I knew it to be the truth.

I have often heard it said that Bruce was so successful because he had natural inborn talent—his speed, his power was only a matter of having the right genes. Bruce's father, Lee Hoi Chuen, was an actor in the Chinese opera, therefore Bruce had a natural affinity for the dramatic arts; Bruce was born with the right structural components, therefore he had a superb physique. The story goes that Bruce didn't really have to work very hard to achieve great things because he had it all from the beginning. Nothing could be further from the truth.

It is not my purpose to enter into a debate about genetics versus environment; certainly they both play a role. My intention is to acquaint the reader with the notion that Bruce Lee did indeed work very hard to build an incredible body, to hone his martial arts skills, to perfect the craft of acting. The most important component of this formula for success, however, was Bruce's self-determination.

This quality of being a self-starter is not something that people either have or don't have. It is a learned characteristic. Bruce achieved a high level of self-motivation through meticulous study of books from Norman Vincent Peale's *Power of Positive Thinking* to Miyamoto Musashi's *Book of Five Rings*. He read, underlined, and made notes in literally hundreds of motivational books. He wrote out in longhand his pledges and goals. He did not look at failure as failure, per se, but as a motivation to rethink his strategies. And failures did happen, such as when all his hopes and his meager bank account were bet on making *The Silent Flute* with James Coburn and Stirling Silliphant. When it did not pan out, this failed project became the immediate impetus to accept the offer in Hong Kong that led to *The Big Boss* and the string of successful films that propelled Bruce to stardom. One of the hardest things for anyone to do in their lives is to pick themselves up off the floor, grab those bootstraps, and reach for that brass ring with the only kick in the pants being self-determination. Bruce used to say, "To hell with opportunity; I *create* opportunity." When he said it, I knew that it would happen.

Bruce turned his search for the best within himself into a virtual art form. Focus was the key, being centered and possessing an infallible awareness of where he was at all times. Bruce did not spend one precious second of his short time on earth reflecting on negative justification—no self-pity, no blaming others for things that didn't go right in his life, no harmful self-indulgence to tempt him from his chosen path. He did not baby himself: he plunged into the unknown future fearlessly but well armed. However, lest you think this was a journey of self-sacrifice and torture, it was not. If there was one thing with which Bruce was naturally blessed, it was the sheer love of what he was doing. He loved martial arts, fitness training, acting, writing, studying. This in itself is truly a gift.

In filmmaking, one principle that Bruce understood well was the necessity for the story line to have a hook—something that grabs the attention of the audience. When it came to keeping his own attention focused, Bruce employed very tangible hooks. He posted motivational sayings and posters around the house; he had a plaque on his desk that said WALK ON; he wrote his goals down on paper and revised them frequently; he envisioned the success he would one day enjoy. But the most tangible,

ever-present reminder was that old broken pair of glasses. With them perched on his face during the lean years, Bruce would look in the mirror and swear that the day would come when he could easily replace his glasses. Later, when he had reached that goal, he used the glasses to motivate himself toward the attainment of new dreams.

That decrepit, battered pair of glasses represented to Bruce the stumbling blocks that he would turn into stepping stones. He used to say, "When you look at a beautiful lake shimmering in the first blush of daybreak, think of the source." Bruce always had a keen awareness of himself and his place in the universe.

Even now, more than two decades after his death, like a long-extinguished star whose light still makes its way to earth, Bruce Lee's star continues to shine, lighting the way for many who would follow in his footsteps.

Linda Lee Cadwell

LINDA LEE CADWELL

Newton's Three Laws of Motion

1. A body at rest remains eternally at rest, and a body at motion remains eternally in uniform motion unless acted upon by an external force

When we stop, a push, a blow or a kick. we receive resistance from them. This resistance is called INERTIA

(Thus, to give motion to a body at rest or to stop a body in motion, we must overcome the inertia of that body)

—— seluтом gap of exertion ——

FORCE :— an action to overcome the inertia of a body.

DEFENSE :
a) to lead opponent to the directio of his exertion, bridging harmoniou
b) to be insubstantial to opponen line of exertion

ATTACK : — MOMENTUM :— the product of the mass of an object times its veloc

[In order to apply a large force momentum in your opponent in the time possible, as well as make n power express your "whole weig enlarge the velocity so that pow velocity can become greater]

The broken rhythm way :—

not to move against but to lead whether one's aura

proper position is a matter of effective inertia organization

1). First of all you must have a "sensitively cool" aura

2). Your footwork must be light and smooth —— extremely fast

3). to have opponent fully commit and out of form

4). to have the "½ beat" to fit in harmoniously either to :—
  a). attack on ungarded mass without momentum
  b). to merge and gap into a single functioning unit
    1. to throw 2. to un-crisp

5). to co-ordinate all power to attack his weakness [the body is soft while the looks are powerful, momentum ; muscular force a stiff and inflexible body is not dynamic, and fail to communicate impetus to opponent's body

Bruce at seven years of age.

Bruce at four or five, pouting.

Bruce and his brother Peter in 1945 as pint-size warriors with swords. Peter went on to become a fencing champion. His interest in the sport was passed on to his brother.

Introduction

Unlike most of our present-day icons of action and adventure, their every career move charted by highly paid retinues of specialists, strategists, and advisors, Bruce Lee essentially constructed himself.

Show business professionals, smooth Armani-clad denizens of power-lunching, expense-account Hollywood, may be horrified to learn that throughout his career Bruce Lee maintained no personal publicist, nor did he even have an agent when he made his wildly popular Hong Kong movies. A lifetime of intense physical training had inclined him toward minding his own career himself.

But he was no babe in the Tinseltown woods either. Although born in San Francisco in 1940—the Year of the Dragon—while his father, Lee Hoi Chuen, a star of the venerable Chinese opera, was in the United States on tour, accompanied by his Eurasian wife, Grace, Bruce Lee was raised in Hong Kong, surrounded by film and opera people and other artists. He appeared in movies there from early childhood on through late adolescence.

By the time he was a teenager, Lee Siu Lung, or "Lee Little Dragon," as he was known in Hong Kong, had appeared in more than twenty Cantonese-language pictures, including *The Orphan,* touted as a Chinese *Blackboard Jungle,* in which he starred.

In many of his early movies, young Lee was typecast as a tough little street urchin who could cartwheel and do back flips and already could use his fists like a miniature adult.

He grew to be an uncommonly focused and disciplined man, one who read widely and incorporated elements of many Western as well as Eastern traditions into jeet kune do, usually translated as "the way of the inter-

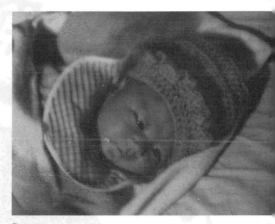

Bruce at two months.

Bruce held by his father at three months. Bruce is made up for his first Cantonese-language film. When he returned to Hong Kong as a young man, Cantonese films were no longer being made even though Hong Kong had a predominantly Cantonese-speaking population.

cepting fist." It became his own "antisystem" of martial art, with which he directly challenged some of the most dearly and closely held beliefs of the martial arts establishment. Lee not only walked the walk, but—to reverse the customary street slang—he talked the talk, and well, too, writing it all down in a measured longhand with calligraphic precision. He himself summed up his warrior's philosophy in a pithy two-word phrase resonant with Zenlike detachment, a phrase also reflective of the young man in a hurry who would not be denied:

Walk on.

Bruce's parents, Grace and Lee Hoi Chuen.

B.L.F.C.

Portraits of the young actor.

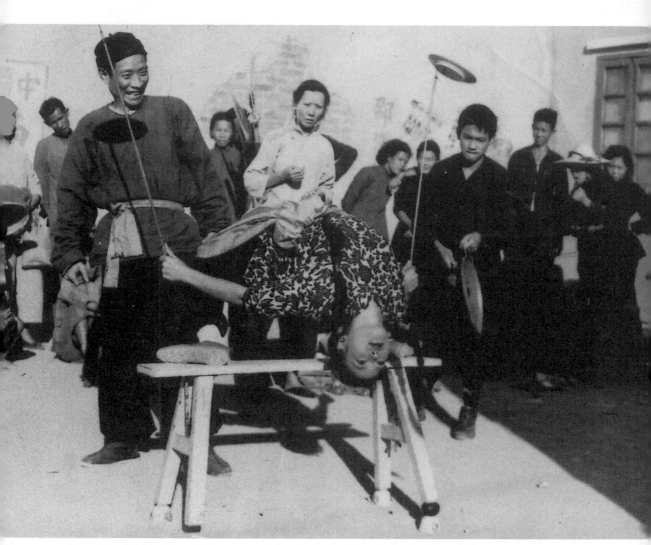

Bruce (at right) intently watching an acrobatic display of plate-spinning in this early film.

Bruce emoting with script while dubbing sound.

At seventeen Bruce was cast in the movie *The Orphan*. It was the last movie he made before leaving Hong Kong for the United States.

YIP MAN
and
THE HONG KONG KID

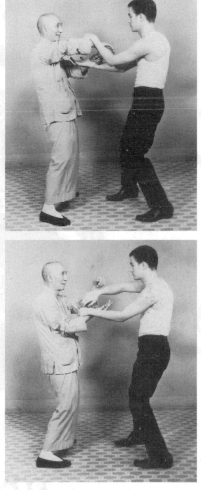

Bruce practicing chi sao (the art of the sticking hand) with Yip Man in Hong Kong in 1963.

A ny sensitive, well-brought-up Chinese kid in Hong Kong in the fifties—then the mercantile southern Chinese outpost of the British empire as well as the capitalist West's window on the "mysterious" communist East—could not help but be troubled by British-Chinese social class conflicts and the cold war tensions of the era. Not surprising, then, that young Bruce Lee, by all accounts a proud and popular lad, got into his share of scrapes and fights growing up in this British Crown Colony. Hot-tempered, fierce, pugnacious—that was how he thought of himself as a teenager, and that was how others saw him as well. Like those of many other bright and curious teenage boys, Lee's indifferent grades reflected his boredom with the strict academic routines of his Catholic high school.

He was a voracious reader, though. He liked to draw and possessed a good eye and a steady hand. He liked movement, too—the body's means of expression—and he took to the tai chi his father practiced, as well as to the dance steps he most probably first learned from his mother, with a young athlete's natural grace.

At the age of thirteen he began to study wing chun, an ancient Chinese martial art. His teacher was the legendary kung fu master Yip Man, who taught the art of detachment as much as he taught the art of unarmed combat, and soon Lee, gifted with grace and ability, became his most prized pupil.

From Master Yip, Lee learned such traditional but unique wing chun methods as chi sao, "the art of the sticking hand," in which practitioners in effect "fence" with their hands and forearms. Practicing chi sao with Yip Man, the young Lee was strengthening himself and sharpening

Bruce and his martial arts mentor, Yip Man, in 1958.

his sense of touch while learning to release an "energy" that he later compared to "floating" an opponent's attack, likening it to an ever-flowing stream or a boat on waves.

From Master Yip he also first learned about Zen and the Tao, and that "there is no conquering, struggling, or dominating," as he wrote later. "The best example . . . is water. Water can penetrate the hardest granite because it is yielding. One cannot stab or strike at water and hurt it, because that which offers no resistance cannot be overcome."

The "empty-mindedness" he learned from the practice of chi sao, Lee wrote later, "applies to all activities . . . such as dancing. If the dancer has any idea at all of displaying his art well, he ceases to be a good dancer, for his mind 'stops' with every movement."

For Lee, as well as for his master, water, always flowing, was a central metaphor for the correct practice of kung fu. Said Master Yip, "A man should always think of the source of the water as he drinks it."

Though little known in this country, Master Yip was the seminal fighting influence for Lee. Yip Man taught a style named after a teenage girl who lived in eighteenth-century China. When fifteen-year-old Yim Wing Chun's father was wrongfully accused of a crime, the dutiful daughter fled her native province with him. Eventually, she was befriended by Ng Mui, formerly an abbess of the Shaolin Monastery, traditionally a powerful center of martial arts teachings. To teach combat skills in Manchu China, though, was to risk the wrath of the emperor, who saw the Shaolin monks as a rival power center and potential fomenters of rebellion. Through guile and deception the monastery eventually was destroyed by the fearful emperor's troops, and the abbess herself became a fugitive. She taught the beautiful young girl, who while in hiding with her father was being harassed by local suitors, to defend herself.

Yip Man holding baby Brandon, July 21, 1965.

An outstanding student, Wing Chun eventually defeated her tormentors in combat. After she married, Wing Chun taught her husband fighting skills; he, in turn, passed them on. From Leung Bok Chau, Wing Chun's husband, to Wong Wah Bo, who was a member of an opera troupe, and on to Leung Jan, an herbal doctor, master passed the techniques on to master, each weaving new strands of technique into the system. Eventually this wing chun system was passed down to Yip Man, who became its grand master in a direct line of succession from the young girl who was the founder. He taught Bruce Lee. After Master Yip's death, the line of succession finally fragmented.

Stories, some probably apocryphal, abound of young Bruce Lee's martial arts prowess, and in many ways the image of the Hong Kong schoolboy is the same as that of the street-brawling tough kid he played in his many Cantonese films. Was he tormented by racist British schoolboys, and did he return from wing chun practice, like some avenging loner from one of his films, to beat them

up, one by one? Did he rise to head one of Hong Kong's ubiquitous youth gangs, battling his rivals across rooftops with fists and sticks? Did a youthful dispute with the son of the leader of one of the Chinese Triads, traditional criminal gangs that wielded power in Hong Kong equivalent to that of the Italian Mafia in Sicily, lead to his death years later? Were the increasingly frequent and violent confrontations, including a run-in with the Hong Kong police, the reason his father sent him back to his birthplace, San Francisco, or was it simply that to retain his American citizenship young Bruce needed to return to his country of birth before his eighteenth birthday? Here the myth melds with reality, but three things are certain.

As a Hong Kong high school student, Bruce Lee won a multischool boxing tournament, defeating the reigning champion. Years later, Bruce would admit that the first time he'd ever laced on a pair of boxing gloves was when he entered this tournament. He was merely putting into practice his wing chun training, but it was the beginning of a lifelong interest in the sport, leading him later, for example, to watch Muhammad Ali's fight films in a mirror, so he could learn the boxer's moves while reversing his left-hand lead.

At the age of eighteen, the young martial artist with a dancer's grace and a natural actor's dramatic style was crowned the Cha-Cha Champion of the Crown Colony. In his repertoire at the time were over a hundred different dance steps.

And in 1959, with the list of one hundred and eight steps neatly printed in tiny longhand on a card he kept in his wallet, Bruce Lee set sail for the United States. In his pocket he carried a hundred dollars from his father. He'd booked passage in steerage for the two-and-a-half-week voyage over, but the ship's crew regularly brought him up to swanky first class, where he could teach dancing to smitten female passengers. But always when a day's lessons were ended, he had to return to his poorer quarters and the lower decks.

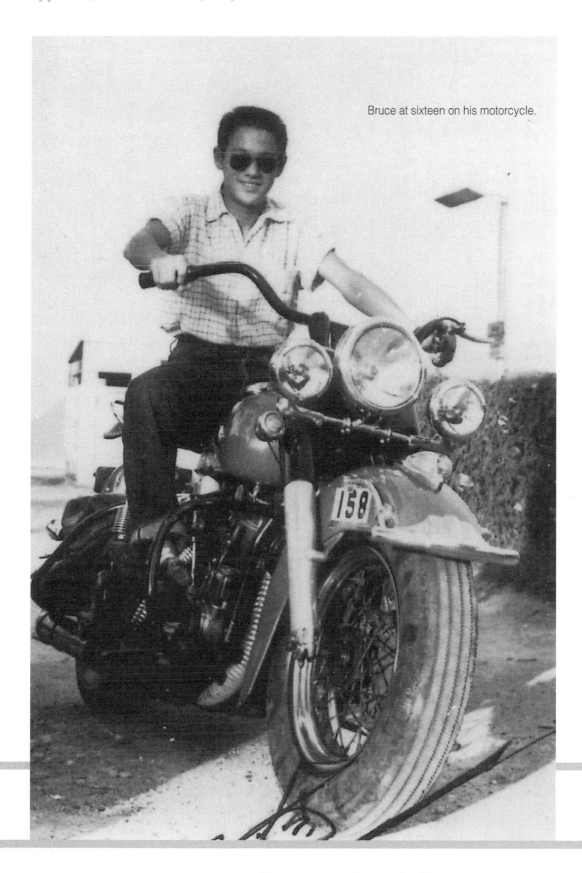

Bruce at sixteen on his motorcycle.

Bruce with a high-collared jacket posing for a school photograph.

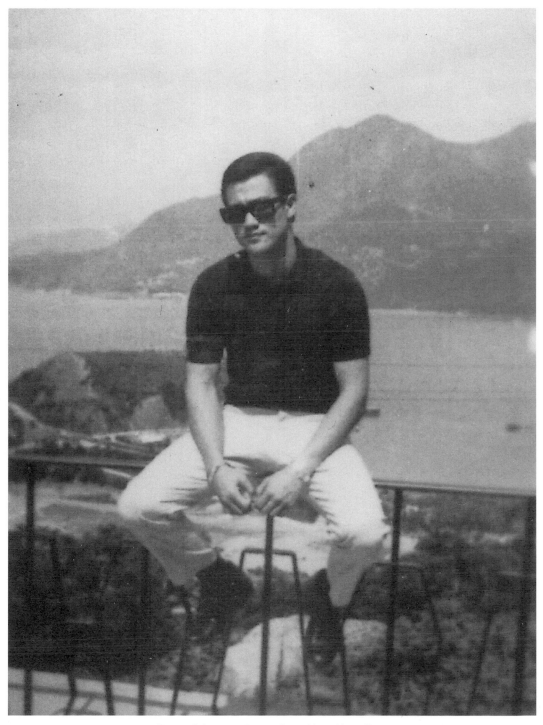

Bruce sitting on a fence above Hong Kong Bay.

Bruce practicing the art of chi sao on bamboo reeds.

Carrying a Scandinavian Airlines flight bag, Bruce poses for a picture during one of his hikes.

Bruce (left) and his brother Peter.

Bruce wearing "Coke-bottle glasses" similar to the pair that later became a symbol of his years of youthful struggle.

Celebration on the deck of the ship prior to departing for the United States on April 29, 1959. Bruce's inscription on the back of the original photograph reads: "Wed. 10 o'clock."

Bruce was an avid dancer, as shown in these shots. It was perhaps this interest in movement that led him to the further discipline of martial arts.

Examples of entries in Bruce's notebook displaying his interest in dancing and the various steps he disciplined himself to learn.

40).	Wave step	60).	Wishbone turn
41).	Circle Step	61).	Break parallel
42).	"A" step	62).	Right angled step
43).	"B" step	63).	Simple kick
44).	"C" Step	64).	Catch collar
45).	Turning Step	65).	Simple roll
46).	Rubbing & scratching	66).	Hop Step
	"Jug" Step	67).	Cross step A
47).	Duck Step	68).	" " B
48).	Samba step	69).	Elvis Presley
49).	Two full turn	70).	Come in
50).	Mixed step	71).	Bicycle step
51).	Basket ball	72).	Twin step
52).	Charleston St.	73).	Half turn
53).	Double step	74).	Quarter turn
54).	One two step	75).	Technique step
55).	Simple step	76).	" " B
56).	Break step	77).	" " C
57).	Quarter break	78).	" " D
58).	Single step	79).	Men & women
59).	Three count	80).	Zig zag step

81).	Basic chicken
82).	Cross chicken
83).	Dn cross step
84).	" full step

Fancy Steps of Cha Cha

1)	Number one	20)	"Poof" step
2)	Number two	21)	Kick Step
3)	Number three	22)	Pull Step
4)	Number four	23)	"R" Step
5)	" five	24)	Eighth Step
6)	" six	25)	" 2 step go
7)	" seven	26)	" 4 "
8)	" eight	27)	Two Step style
9)	New Step A	28)	Three "
10)	" B	29)	Number 4 with 38th
11)	Change	30)	Rubbing & double
12)	Changing Step	31)	
13)	Slide Step	32)	
14)	Square Step	33)	"R" side pull
15)	Tango Step	34)	New half turn
16)	Three steps back	35)	Salty Step
17)	Banana boat	36)	Manila Style
18)	Walking Step	37)	Side Step

THE EASTERN PHILOSOPHER
and
THE ALL-AMERICAN GIRL

From the first time she saw him, Linda Emery thought Bruce Lee looked like a dashing character from a movie. That film was *West Side Story* and the character he reminded her of was Bernardo, played by George Chakiris, to be exact.

It was 1963. She was seventeen, pretty, blond, and vivacious—the type who put sugar in her Chinese tea, she says now of her youthful self. She and her girlfriends had just seen the acclaimed movie musical, based on the Broadway play that was in turn loosely based on *Romeo and Juliet*. They'd gushed over the exotic, darkly handsome Bernardo, charismatic leader of the Sharks, the Puerto Rican gang in the film. Bernardo, tragic Maria's older brother, was old-fashioned and macho, a hot-blooded character with a glare and a sneer, someone who settled turf disputes with his fists.

It was he who she immediately thought of when an older student, a twenty-one-year-old studying philosophy, newly enrolled at the University of Washington, came to Garfield High School to give a lecture on Eastern philosophy.

She wasn't in the class herself, but she remembers "it was kind of like a celebrity event when this guy, a college student, came to give lectures in a high school philosophy class."

Her girlfriends would see him and stage whisper to each other, "Look, there's that Bruce Lee guy."

Bruce Lee had been in the United States almost four years, and in his progress, he embodied the traditional image of the hardworking immigrant in America. From San Francisco he'd soon come north to Seattle. He studied and worked hard, reading avidly and perfecting his

Bruce in the United States with his newly purchased clothes posing in front of a stylish new De Soto.

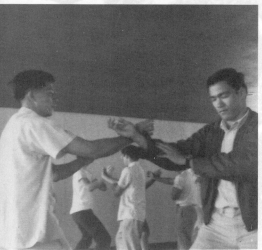

Bruce teaching a self-defense class.

martial arts skills; took any odd jobs that came his way, such as the one at Ruby Chow's restaurant, where he learned to make wontons and above which he boarded; and he saved his money. Teaching kung fu to eager young Americans, it soon became apparent, was preferable to cooking and washing dishes in a Chinese restaurant.

After the Second World War, veterans returning from occupation duty in and around Japan had brought back with them to America a mostly rudimentary knowledge of judo and karate, but by the early sixties the traditional Eastern arts of unarmed combat in general, and kung fu (or gung fu, as it is also pronounced) in particular, were still mostly unknown to the general public. Martial arts instruction was just beginning to spread out from such port cities as Seattle, Oakland, San Francisco, Los Angeles, and Long Beach, where communities of returning veterans were centered. In fact, an informal but widely honored prohibition then existed among many Asian masters not to teach the more advanced combat methods to Westerners.

In Seattle, young Bruce Lee—hip, brash, and increasingly Americanized—already was upsetting all of that. For a University of Washington fraternity's Fight Night program in 1960, for example, he gave a Chinese boxing–judo exhibition. His crisp demonstrations and engaging manner attracted students, who at first practiced in a large parking garage on Sundays, when the cars weren't there, then later in a dimly lighted basement.

Linda Emery had a Chinese girlfriend at Garfield High who studied with the glamorous college student. She remembers it as "so strange. Nobody had ever heard of kung fu, hardly even karate back in those days."

The summer before she started college herself, she began to join her friend in Chinatown. "You had to go down a dark stairs to a cement cellar with one lightbulb in it and that's where the classes were, so it was intriguing."

After the lessons, the entire group would go out to a

Chinese restaurant or to a Chinese- or Japanese-language movie, particularly if it was one of the long-running *Zatoichi* series, one of Bruce's favorites, about a wandering blind swordsman. His adventures always expertly blended action and comedy.

Before long, Bruce Lee opened a school near the university, where he taught the techniques of martial arts as he'd learned them from Yip Man, direct successor in the line of unarmed-combat mastery that stretched back to the Shaolin Temple: the straight punch, the elbows in, the straight line—all wing chun staples.

Bruce demonstrating a defense tactic to Taky Kimura. At right is Linda. Taky Kimura was Bruce's best man at his wedding.

Bruce practicing in Hong Kong in 1963 with Doug Palmer, a student from Seattle.

But to the time-honored training, he also was beginning to add his own borrowings and innovations. Along with the kung fu repertoire of kicks and punches, his students were learning judo throws. He himself learned from old boxing fight films and from the biographies of past champs, just as he learned from his readings in science and philosophy, from Newton to Descartes to Hume, adapting both Western physical and metaphysical principles to the martial arts.

Always he taught mental attitude and relaxation, "stillness" and economy of means.

The school was wildly successful, and he began to formulate something new, a forceful combination of warrior training methods and, more important, a new way of *perceiving* the martial arts. Although he steadfastly resisted all attempts to label it as a new martial art, others consider this the first martial arts system created in America. Eventually he named it jeet kune do, "the way of the intercepting fist," and it was, he emphasized, more about mind than muscle. Meanwhile, Bruce and Linda had begun to date.

She remembers that, one day, "he kind of had me tackled in a throw, he'd thrown me on the ground, and he said, 'Would you like to go to the Space Needle?' I said, 'You mean, *all* of us go to the Space Needle?'

"He said, 'No, just you.' Ooooh!"

She remembers, too, exactly what he wore on their first date, "because he looked so dapper. He wore a black Italian suit with a purple shirt."

The date was October 25, 1963. "That was when we kind of paired off. . . . We just spent a lot of time together from then on."

Both he and Linda talked candidly in public on several occasions over the years about the difficulties of an interracial romance in the America of the mid-sixties. One of the many poems he penned around that time seems to speak directly to the issue:

Once more, again, I hold you in my arms;
And once more I lost myself in
A paradise of my own.
Right now you and I are in
A golden boat drifting freely on a sunny sea
Far, far away from the human world.
I am happy as the waves dancing around us.

Too much analysis kills spontaneity,
As too much light dazzles my eyes.
Too much truth astonishes me.
Despite all obstacles,
Love still exists between us.

It is useless to try to stir the dirt
Out of the muddy water,
As it will become murkier.
But leave it alone,
And if it should be cleared,
It will become clear by itself.

Left: Bruce teaching a class in self-defense.

Right: Hong Kong tai chi practice in 1963. Bruce's father is second from right, and Bruce himself is fourth from the right.

After spending several months back in Hong Kong in 1963, Bruce returned briefly to Seattle before moving down to Oakland, where he opened a second school. Two weeks later, in August 1964, Bruce Lee and Linda Emery were married. Taky Kimura, his first student in Seattle and a friend of long standing, who eventually took over leadership of the Seattle school, was their best man.

Before the marriage, Linda's family hadn't known about her romance with a Chinese-American man. "It caused

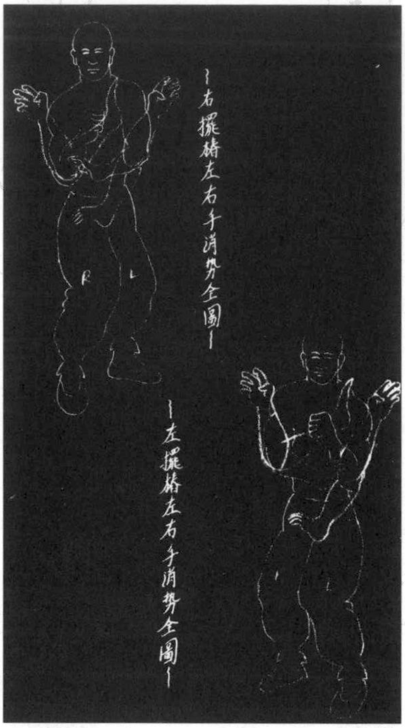

Two renditions of the eight basic blocking positions hand drawn by Bruce.

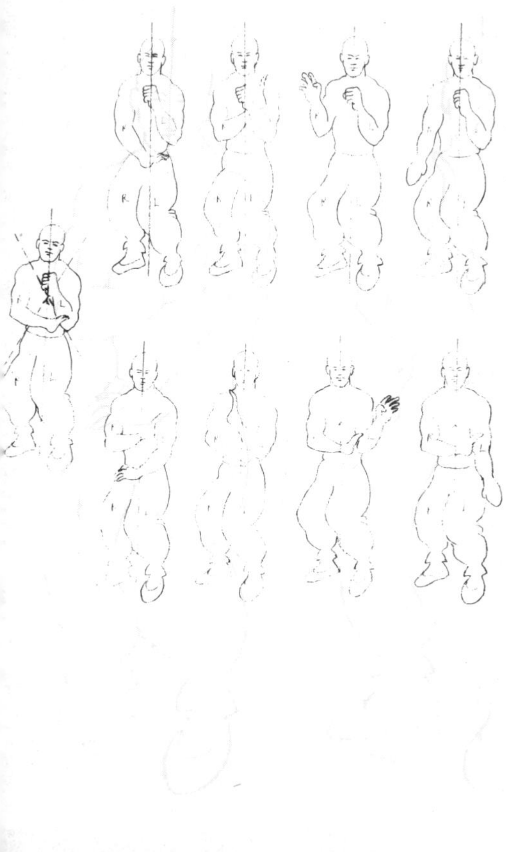

quite a disruption in my family," she remembers. "To their credit they wanted the best for me, [but] felt I was hopelessly complicating my life by marrying a person of another race." As for herself, she says simply that she looked at Bruce Lee "straight across as another human being."

Within the insular martial arts world, Bruce Lee seemed well on the way to a life of local celebrity and some controversy as the brash Young Turk of kung fu. His caustic public pronouncements about board- and brick-breaking tricks and about the dubious usefulness of kata, as well as of other ancient and enshrined techniques taught by rote repetition, in actual life-and-death encounters out in the real world of sudden violence and street fighting, enraged the establishment.

More than once, "masters" of other styles or tournament champions took offense and disparaged him in public, about everything from his controversial "one-inch punch" (actually, a demonstration of the power of applied "focus") to his unabashed willingness to teach martial arts secrets to Caucasians, only to study with him later in private.

A kung-fu master recently arrived in the United States challenged Lee to battle over the teaching Caucasians issue, according to one famous story. When Lee obliged, the master was so badly beaten that he fled.

According to another widely known story, a karate expert who insisted on a full-contact confrontation had to be carried away unconscious afterward, only to return to become one of Bruce Lee's students. The stories of Lee's fighting prowess spread around the circuit, and the controversies only added to his growing fame.

Then Bruce Lee, the charismatic young master, gave a demonstration in the summer of 1964 at a Long Beach karate tournament organized by the famed kempo instructor Ed Parker, who numbered Elvis Presley among his students and is often referred to as the father of modern American karate, and suddenly everything changed.

Bruce working with the makiwara board dummy. Bruce added a leg to the traditional workout dummy.

Bruce at the airport, returning to Hong Kong from the
United States in 1963. His parents are on the left.

Bruce proudly displays his ROTC uniform, which he acquired
at the University of Washington.

Left: Various defense movements shot in Hong Kong in 1963. The arrows were added by Bruce.

Opposite: The infamous "one-inch punch." Rivals often disparaged Lee's one-inch punch unless they were on the other end of it and felt its power. Notice that the karate man (right) has been caught by the camera immediately after the blow, with his heels off the floor, just as he's about to be knocked back into the waiting chair.

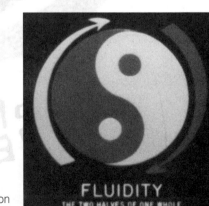

The flowing arrows are Bruce's own addition to the traditional yin-yang symbol.

FLUIDITY
THE TWO HALVES OF ONE WHOLE

Bruce in his Kato mask and hat.

SMALL SCREEN, BIG IMPACT

Bruce Lee's reputation, like that of James Dean, whom Lee admired, is based on a relatively small body of work. Despite his career as a child actor in Hong Kong, as an adult he was a regular on just one American TV series, *The Green Hornet,* which aired for only one twenty-six-episode season in the mid-sixties, and he starred in just five martial arts films, including one completed by stand-ins and released in 1978, five years after his death.

Still, nearly a quarter of a century later, he remains the internationally recognized on-screen avatar of athletic grace and unparalleled martial art.

In 1993, his star was added to the Hollywood Walk of Fame. When *Dragon,* a big-screen, Hollywood studio Bruce Lee biopic starring Jason Scott Lee (no relation, despite his last name), was released that year, it opened at number one, taking in ten million dollars at the box office, the biggest opening to that date on the traditionally slow first weekend in May. Similarly, when the Arts & Entertainment cable channel's *Biography* did an hour on Lee, it became one of the top-five–rated episodes of that series ever to air. And when his son Brandon's last movie, the posthumously released *The Crow,* opened, it too debuted in first place at the box office.

Steven Seagal, Jean-Claude Van Damme, Chuck Norris, and Jackie Chan notwithstanding, there has been no "new" Bruce Lee; arguably the closest and most charismatic incarnation thus far was Brandon Lee, whose own promising career was cut off even earlier than his father's in its upward arc.

How then to account for the continuing interest and the myth? While the art is timeless, the life is fixed forever in a specific, and unique, time. Lee came to pop-star

The James Dean pose.

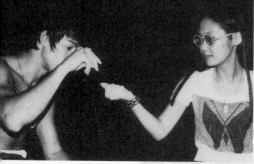

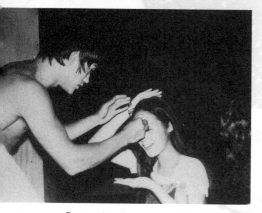

Bruce showing a young fan his famous coin trick in the early 1970s.

prominence in the late sixties and early seventies, the era of Vietnam and counterculture, of moon shots and disco. Hollywood was rediscovering the huge baby-boomer market, as its strategists had been doing periodically ever since the era of coonskin caps and Hula Hoops. The boomers were ready for a new kind of hero, even though Hollywood moguls might have preferred the tried-and-true.

As always in Hollywood, however, it was the job of the professionals to read the signs and ride the waves. Producer William Dozier, who'd begun the craze of reviving radio serials from the thirties and forties for TV with the camp mid-sixties version of *Batman,* was looking for someone to play the offspring of private-eye Charlie Chan in *Number One Son,* a projected series that never materialized. His celebrity hairdresser Jay Sebring, who later was one of the victims in the notorious Tate–La Bianca Manson killings, raved about a young man he'd seen recently doing a martial arts demonstration at a Long Beach, California, karate tournament, according to one version of the story. As it happened, the organizer of the tournament had filmed the demonstration.

Dozier took one look at the film and knew that here was his Number One Son. He brought the twenty-four-year-old martial artist and former child actor to Hollywood for a screen test, for which Lee appeared in a dark suit and tie.

Seated in a chair on a nondescript interior set, poised, confident, and alert with his hands clasped over one knee, Lee looked matinee-idol handsome. He was patient with his officious offscreen interlocutor, even when, like some X-ray technician, he asked Lee to turn in three-quarter profile and "Hold it."

Just seated, immobile, Lee fascinated the camera, but he came startlingly alive when he stood up and began demonstrating crisp, lightning-quick kung fu moves on a portly, bespectacled volunteer from backstage. Of the

volunteer, who kept nervously flinching as punches and kicks exploded inches from his head, Lee deadpanned that he looked "kinda worried."

Dozier immediately put the dynamic, charismatic young man under a one-year contract, and though the Charlie Chan series fell through, when *The Green Hornet* got the green light, Dozier had his Kato waiting.

The Green Hornet, in which newspaperman Britt Reid (played on TV by Van Williams) and his chauffeur-sidekick Kato don masks to fight crime, was based on a popular thirties radio show created by George Trendle and Fran Striker, who also had created *The Lone Ranger.* In fact, their original scripts made the connection between the Ranger and the Hornet explicit: Britt Reid's great-grandfather *was* the Lone Ranger.

But Bruce Lee was dubious. Kato was a Japanese name, but in the original radio series, his ancestry had been reduced to vaguely "Oriental" (as a post–Pearl Harbor gesture of wartime political correctness) and he'd been relegated to chores as a houseboy. Would he be reduced to a pigtail-wearing, pidgin-speaking Tonto clone, and did the world really need another Asian stereotype?

Still, it was the sixties and rebellion and consciousness-raising were in the air. In addition, his own life was moving on. He and Linda had a newborn son, Brandon, and the same week he was born, Bruce's father died in Hong Kong. Bruce Lee had new family responsibilities, and perhaps this Kato would have something of the spirit of the times.

He didn't get the part because of his acting or fighting skills, he took to joking ruefully to the press, but because he was the only Chinese person in California who could pronounce "Britt Reid." In fact, as it turned out—from "Beautiful Dreamer," the premiere episode, onward through such installments as "Deadline for Death," "The Preying Mantis," and "The Ray Is for Killing" (in which the bad guys employ a laser-beam "death ray")—he rarely

The front of Bruce's business membership cards.

截拳道精華

訪問李小龍的老師

截拳道精神——
以無限爲有限
以無法爲有法

蓮達談李小龍

截拳道菁華錄

李小龍示範自衞散手

was given more to do than pronounce his on-screen employer's name and show how well this Kato could Chinese box.

"Roll it, Kato!" the Hornet would boom, and they would dash off yet again in the Black Beauty, their tricked-out mid-sixties supercar, to fight evil and crime.

Not surprisingly, behind the wheel, with his masked employer comfortably at ease in the backseat, Kato sometimes wore an expression of faint amusement or even slight chagrin.

The otherwise undistinguished 20th Century-Fox Television series, which aired on Friday nights opposite *The Wild Wild West* and a Tarzan series, was part of a short-lived action-adventure-satire trend on sixties television that included *Batman*, Dozier's other series, and *West*. They all shared a pop-art look and a camp sensibility.

But for the young fans, it was Kato who kicked through the screen. Lee choreographed his own fight scenes, and not surprisingly they were the high point of each *Green Hornet* show. For once, the show-business cliché proved true: "overnight," Bruce Lee, who was barely even given a line of dialogue on TV beyond "Britt Reid residence," became a grassroots youth sensation.

The fan mail, much of it from young girls, and the requests for personal appearances came pouring in. A group of businessmen approached him with a scheme to commit his popularity to franchising Kato Schools of Self-Defense, but the young actor, who certainly could have used the quick infusion of money, refused, observing that there could be no quality control of the instruction offered at the schools, which merely would be trading on his image and his TV name.

Unlike many other rising young actors whose success breeds seclusion and an arrogant attitude, Bruce remained at ease, loquacious, and witty. "Can you dig it?" "dude," "man," "far out," and other with-it interjections of the time peppered his casual conversation. Not surprisingly, he became a favorite of the press, which took to focusing on him in their *Green Hornet* coverage, writing awed, glowing stories that typically described him as "charming" and a "complete ham."

He was both. Sometimes Lee's on-screen movements were so fast that the camera had to film him at a slower speed just to be able to catch the action. And he delighted the fans that flocked to him, as well as the press, with simple coin tricks demonstrating his prowess. He would place a dime in a child's (or a reporter's) open palm. "Close your hand before I can snatch it away," he would say, "and you can keep the dime."

Baby Brandon displaying, perhaps for the first time, his obviously hereditary affinity for kicking.

Once, twice . . . and each time he would grab the dime before the hand could close. A third attempt, and this time his unsuspecting victim could *feel* the coin still caught in his tightly closed hand.

"I've got it!" would come the inevitable triumphant cry. But when the fist slowly opened, it revealed . . .

The dime replaced by a penny!

Lee remained fearless, too, in his criticisms of usually sacrosanct subjects. The show's scripts were generally bad, he said candidly, and the producers were constantly trying to get him to do stunts that would make a travesty of his beloved martial arts. As for showboating martial arts teachers who specialized in precisely such

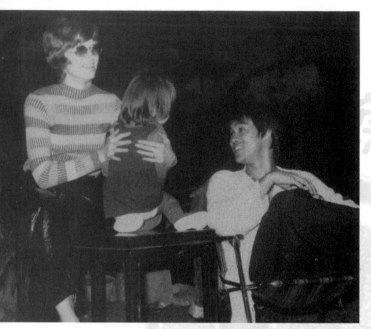

Brandon, Linda, Shannon, and Bruce enjoying a relaxed moment in their backyard in Los Angeles.

Two pages from Bruce's daily journal exhibiting the exercise routine he was practicing at the time. The discipline was similar to that which he had applied to dancing nearly a decade earlier.

tricks, board- and brick-breaking was "just a stunt," he often said. "Boards don't hit back."

The press loved it, and they gleefully reprinted the bad puns to which he was addicted. For example, Lee impishly (and tirelessly) repeated that he didn't drink or smoke, but he did chew gum, because "a lot of men smoke but Fu Manchu."

How was it that the ratings demise of the ill-conceived and indifferently executed *Green Hornet* didn't lead automatically to a better series, created especially for and starring a born media pied piper like Bruce Lee?

Says Linda Lee, "I don't think we experienced a great deal of racism, prejudice, except when it came to Bruce breaking into Hollywood. . . . They didn't think he was a bankable personality. [Years after *The Green Hornet,* they] wouldn't give him the lead in *Kung Fu,* which led to us going to Hong Kong."

True, in the aftermath of the *Hornet,* Lee-as-Kato appeared with Van Williams as a guest star in "A Piece of the Action" and "Batman's Satisfaction," a two-part *Batman* episode about foiling a rare-stamp counterfeiter. And he appeared in the occasional episode of other TV series—*Ironside,* starring Raymond Burr as the wheelchair-bound detective, for example, or *Blondie,* in which he played Dagwood Bumstead's karate teacher in an episode titled "Pick on a Bully Your Own Size."

Hollywood doesn't lead the popular

taste, so much as it—at best—crystalizes it, and while other reasons have been advanced (and some, like the reedy quality of Lee's voice, may even have been legitimate factors), the pervasive and automatic racism of a period during which America was embroiled in an Asian land war was a severe obstacle for any minority actor, much less the first young Chinese actor with crossover appeal, to overcome.

Early in his career Lee remarked to producers that he aspired to a part like Bill Cosby's in the groundbreaking mid-sixties TV series *I Spy*, and that he hoped someday to play a Clint Eastwood-style action-adventure hero on the big screen. In this emerging era of multicultural media, when "Hollywood" broadly construed will encompass a spectrum of Chinese filmmaking from *Eat Drink Man Woman* to the violent screen poetry of John Woo, it may be hard to credit that the response from the show-business "professionals" was one of such dismissive certainty: the American public would *never* accept an Asian as a leading man.

When *The Green Hornet* was canceled, Lee was informed in a flip note from producer Dozier, whose condescending language would be unthinkable today: "Confucius say, *Green Hornet* to buzz no more," Lee said that the note had read.

While the series disappeared into syndication overseas, Lee, whose Chinese birth name was Jun Fan, resumed teaching, opening the Jun Fan Gung Fu Institute in

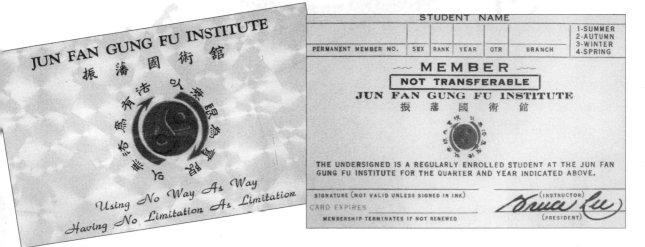

Los Angeles. On a small easel at the front of his desk, Lee placed a small card on which, in a flowing hand, were inscribed just two words: Walk on.

Soon, despite the fact that it bore no identifying sign outside, celebrity students were finding their way to the school in Chinatown, among them prolific film-and-television writer Stirling Silliphant, *Chinatown* director Roman Polanski, Lakers basketball star Kareem Abdul-Jabbar, and such prominent actors of the day as Steve McQueen, Lee Marvin, James Coburn, and James Garner.

If he was disappointed by corporate Hollywood's casual disdain, he never showed it. He walked on, immersing himself in teaching his martial arts and in pursuing a personal program of physical and mental development that was as advanced as it was eclectic.

In combat, he said, "efficiency is anything that scores," and on the wall of his Los Angeles school he hung his observation that the "truth in combat is different for each individual."

Unlike other martial arts instructors, who taught students by sparring with no contact, Lee put on boxing gloves and protective gear and pioneered the practice of full-contact workouts. Anything else, he averred, would be like learning to swim without ever getting into the water.

The elements of his daily physical and nutritional regimen were just as eclectic and results-oriented—everything from taking high-protein drinks and several small meals daily, rather than the traditional three squares, to weight training, practicing kicks on a boxing heavy bag, interval training, and jogging around the streets of West L.A. while wearing hand and leg weights.

He worked out intensely for two or three hours daily, but even after, while reading or watching TV, he would be perpetually flexing or rotating, curling or lifting, stretching or doing isometrics. He bicycled, he shadow-boxed, he skipped rope and worked the speed bag. He mastered the one-finger push-up.

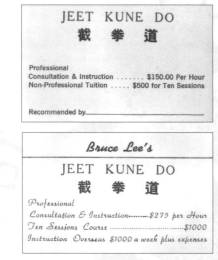

Note how along with the rise in Bruce's popularity and notoriety, his prices rose as well.

This kind of rigorous training program may be familiar (at least as an ideal) to the committed athlete of today, but in the sixties it all was new and startling, and never had a martial artist at Lee's exalted level trained in this way.

He increased his speed and power, honed his reflexes, sharpened every move by sparring, and no one who was there during his drive toward physical perfection ever was able to keep up.

It all came snapping to a sudden stop, though, when he badly damaged a nerve in the sacrum, or lower spine, doing Good Morning, an exercise in which he bent forward from the waist with a heavily weighted barbell on his shoulders.

While recovering from the painful 1970 back injury, Lee, the voracious reader of everything from Krishnamurti to kinesiology and the inveterate student of philosophy and the warrior way, began to commit to paper the principles of his own antisystem of martial art, jeet kune do. Not unexpectedly, he emphasized real-world tactics and drew on martial arts systems as diverse as American boxing, European fencing, and, of course, wing chun.

In April 1969, Bruce and Linda's second child, daughter Shannon, had been born in Santa Monica, California. Back in Seattle, he'd been charging fifteen dollars per month for instruction. Now he was charging his private students in Hollywood two hundred and fifty dollars per hour, or a thousand dollars for ten lessons. As the sixties drew to a close, he was making almost twice as much yearly from giving martial arts lessons as he was from acting and residuals, mostly from *The Green Hornet*.

His back doctors emphasized the seriousness and permanence of the nerve damage, warning him that he'd never do kung fu again, but within six months of his original injury, he was teaching and working out as before. During his painful recuperation, he produced six entire volumes of writings about his way and his art.

IN MEMORY
OF
A ONCE FLUID MAN
CRAMMED AND DISTORTED
BY
THE CLASSICAL MESS

A miniature tombstone displayed in Bruce's Chinatown school.

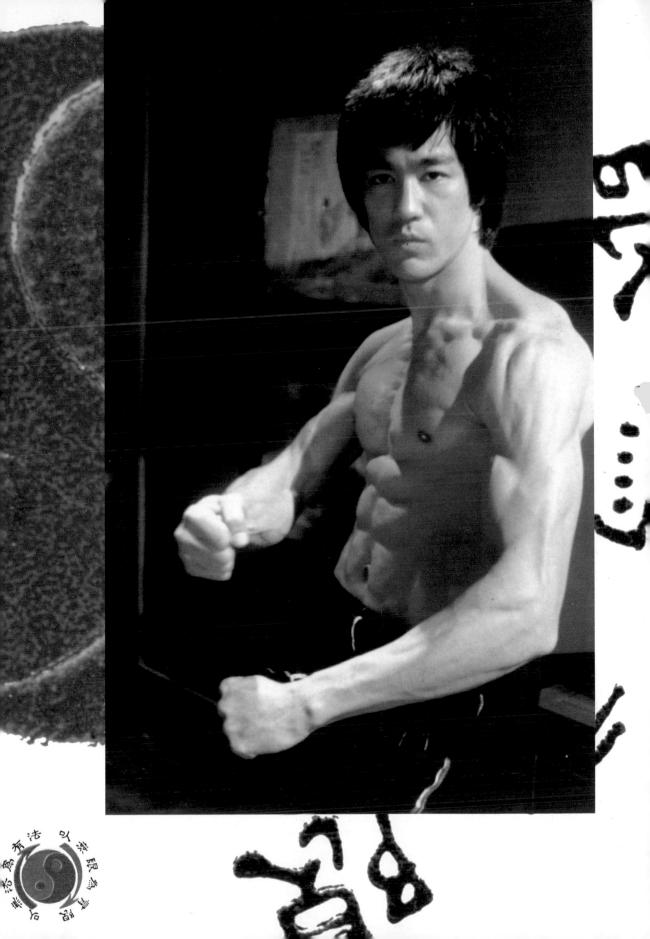

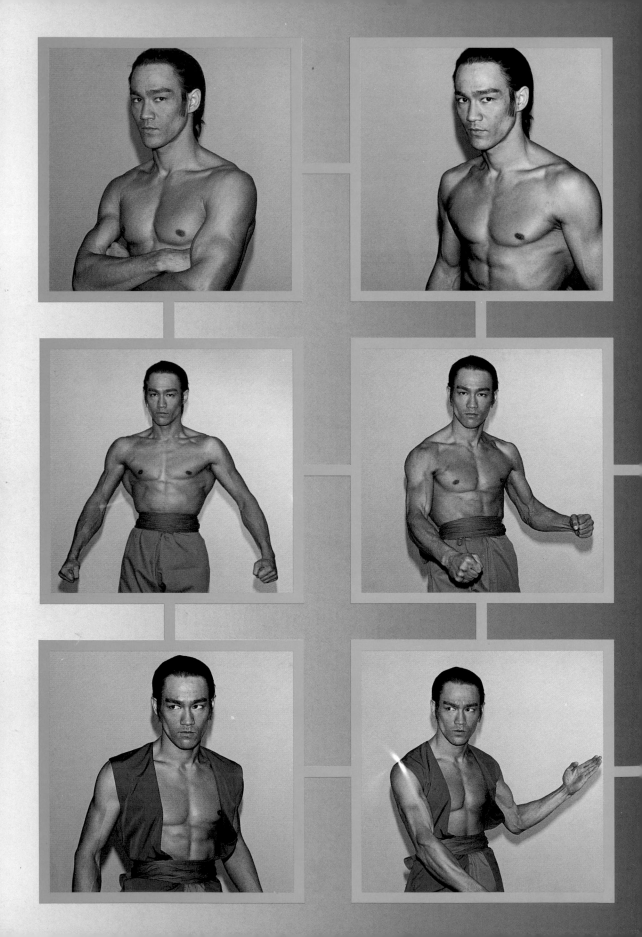

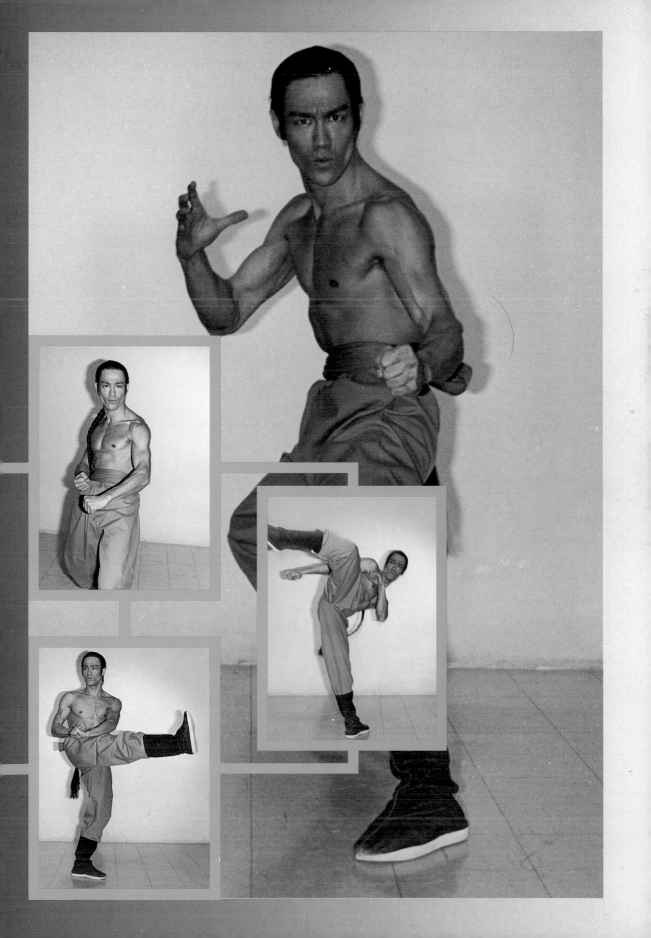

THE TAO
of
HOLLYWOOD

Then as now, Hollywood was the it's-not-*what*-you-know, it's-*who*-you-know town par excellence, and Bruce Lee's next few show-business job opportunities in the late sixties—guest shots on series television, small technical assignments choreographing fight scenes in movies—resulted as much from his network of showbiz students as from his unparalleled skills. What they thought of Bruce Lee in Hong Kong, and elsewhere in Asia, where *The Green Hornet* was still playing, didn't count in Hollywood. Still, each time he appeared in an American role that showcased his action talents, he created a sensation.

But the accolades were no surprise to Lee's hometown fans. In Hong Kong, Singapore, and elsewhere in Asia, his old series, canceled after a single season on American television, was still playing in syndication. And in the Crown Colony, they knew their audience.

It wasn't called *The Green Hornet* there. And while they didn't call it *The Bruce Lee Show* either, they did the next best thing: in Hong Kong *The Green Hornet* was called *Kato.*

At first, Lee was unaware of his popularity in Hong Kong. After all, in America he was simply one more underemployed actor, with a unique, if rather puzzling, skill. But Lee was astute enough to cooperate with studio publicity campaigns, for example hitting the road to tout *Marlowe,* a 1969 picture based on Raymond Chandler's novel *Little Sister* and starring James Garner as cinema's most famous private eye. Lee, in addition to choreographing the film's fight scenes, played the hired-killer villain of the piece, the whimsically named Winslow Wong, who destroys the hero's office with his bare hands

Bruce, Linda, and Brandon celebrating Linda's birthday in March 1967.

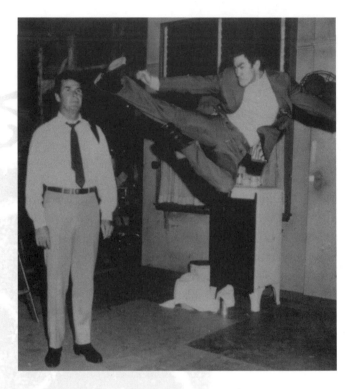

Bruce as Winslow Wong high-kicking the stoic James Garner as Marlowe.

and impossibly high kicks before being killed himself. Deadpanned Lee airily: "Seven hundred million Chinese can't be Wong."

Its flashiness notwithstanding, the role was a bit part, and the sheer fact that the studio would send him out to do publicity (and that, moreover, he would agree to do it) was a testament both to his understanding of the pressure points that move the mighty media machine and to the growing power of his connection with the American press and public.

That connection was reinforced when Lee appeared in *Longstreet,* a new Paramount private-eye TV series written by Lee's student, Stirling Silliphant, who earlier also had adapted the Chandler novel for the big screen. The episode was titled "The Way of the Intercepting Fist"—in other words, jeet kune do—and it told the story of how the blind title character, Mike Longstreet, played by

James Franciscus, had learned fighting skills from the rather reluctant martial arts teacher Lee played.

As always, Lee worked to add texture to his martial-arts-teacher role, to imbue the TV character with the same principles he brought to the role in real life. "I cannot teach you," says his character, echoing Lee himself, "only help you explore yourself. Nothing more."

And later: "I don't believe in system, Mister Longstreet, nor in method. . . . Without system, without method, what is to teach?"

During a demonstration, his character easily blocks an unexpected left jab, explaining, "I intercept your emotional tenseness."

Originally scheduled to be the fourth episode of the new weekly series, "The Way of the Intercepting Fist," with Lee as guest star, so impressed the producers and network executives that they moved the episode up, making it the series debut. Reviews in the trade papers and elsewhere chimed in, praising Lee's performance, and no less than the *New York Times* suggested that here was a personality who'd earned himself his own series.

Sheer talent and charisma were forcing the studios to put Lee-related projects into development. But Lee already had made plans to return to Hong Kong, where he was going to make a Chinese-language film. By the time the American studio had decided it wanted to make him a regular on the series, Lee was in Thailand on location, shooting *The Big Boss,* which eventually became known in the United States as *Fists of Fury,* his first mature Hong Kong–produced film, and offers from other studios, including Warner Bros., were coming in. Eventually, though, he agreed to reprise the character.

When Lee returned to Hollywood, he shot three additional *Longstreet* episodes. Now there were plans in development for a Warner TV series set in the old West to be called *The Warrior* and for a movie, *The Silent Flute,* to be shot in India, where the studio wanted to make use

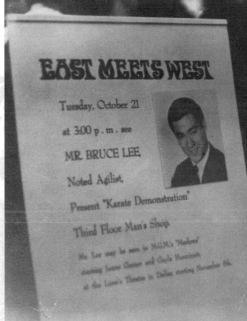

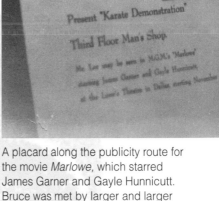

A placard along the publicity route for the movie *Marlowe,* which starred James Garner and Gayle Hunnicutt. Bruce was met by larger and larger crowds as the tour went on.

A snapshot on the location scouting
trip to India for the projected movie
The Silent Flute.

of its cache of local currency that couldn't be taken out of
the country.

Flute, like *The Warrior,* was based on Lee's own con-
cepts, and it sounded what by now were familiar themes
in the young kung fu instructor's life—the same themes
that soon would be sounded worldwide in the Hong
Kong films.

"This is a story of one man's quest for liberation," Lee
wrote of *Flute.* "Unlike the old West's 'fastest gun alive,'
the individual is not out to sharpen his tools to destroy his
antagonist; rather, his side kick . . . etc., are directed pri-
marily toward himself."

Ah Sahm, Lee's *Flute* character, is as dubious about
the value of "styles" and "schools" as was Lee himself.
Says Ah Sahm: "A path and a gateway have no meaning
or use once the objective is in sight."

Of another character's highly disciplined and precise
method of eating his food—a method he'd learned in a
monastery—Ah Sahm observes skeptically that a "hungry

N MAC VICAR
IGTON, D. C.

Bruce at the National Karate Championships organized by Jhoon Rhee. Rhee was a friend of Bruce's and was often called the Father of American tae kwon do.

man, disciplining himself in this manner, might starve to death while still counting [the precise number of chews]."

In America, the men who ran the networks and the studios were dubious, too. America still wasn't ready for an Asian leading man, they decided. *Flute,* which had gotten as far as a location-scouting trip that Lee, James Coburn, and Stirling Silliphant made to the Indian sub-continent, fell through. And the role of Caine, the flute-playing Shaolin monk roaming the old West in the *Warrior* series, went to David Carradine.

Lee made plans to return with his family to Hong Kong. Hollywood wasn't ready for "Hopalong Wong," Lee said wryly of the role that originally had been conceived by him and was written for him in the series that subsequently was retitled *Kung Fu.*

BOSS/FISTS

*T*he *Big Boss* (a.k.a., *Fists of Fury*), costarring Maria Yi and Nora Miao, two popular Hong Kong actresses of the time, was the first of a two-picture deal with Raymond Chow's newly formed Golden Harvest production company.

Chow, the son of the chairman of the Bank of China and a student of kung fu in his youth, had spent more than a decade as head of production for the four Shanghai-born, Mandarin-speaking Shaw brothers, then Asia's most powerful movie moguls, before striking out on his own in 1970. That same year, Lee, ever the savvy promoter, made several appearances on Hong Kong television in connection with the local Kato sensation, and his frequent martial arts demonstrations on *Enjoy Yourself Tonight,* Hong Kong TV's version of *The Tonight Show,* caught Chow's experienced eye.

Bruce applying makeup.

In June 1971, Chow engaged Lee to act in two pictures. Under the original agreement, Bruce Lee would receive the less-than-princely sum of fifteen thousand dollars for doing both.

Like Bruce Lee, who had grown up in it, Raymond Chow knew the rough-and-tumble world of Hong Kong filmmaking, where pictures were sometimes financed by the criminal Triads. Later, when Lee told American reporters about his "overnight" stardom, he often would describe how strangers in Hong Kong suddenly began to press huge amounts of money upon him, telling him "not to worry" about it, that perhaps sometime in the future they might do a picture together. Lee himself never explained the provenance of these generous strangers to the puzzled American journalists, but most likely they were approaches by the Triads wanting to co-opt the new star.

Bruce with a Hong Kong stuntman. He liked Hong Kong stuntpeople because they knew exactly how to stage a dramatic fight on film. During his entire career Bruce campaigned for higher wages for all his stuntpeople.

Bruce with the wife of Lo Wei (director of both *The Big Boss* and *The Chinese Connection*), who was one of the film's producers.

Bruce rehearsing a scene for *The Big Boss*.

Bruce with director Lo Wei.

Hong Kong movies were churned out with dizzying speed in a few short weeks, and shooting usually had to take place at night and early in the morning to avoid the high-decibel noise and constant bustle of the ever-growing city in daytime. Because of the constant noise level, movies shot with scenes in daytime Hong Kong were filmed without sound, with their dialogue and sound effects dubbed in later inside the studio in postproduction.

Hollywood's legions of studio bureaucrats and its pampered megastars of today would be hard put to keep up with the frenzied pace of Hong Kong filmmaking, but the silent era's pioneers, who fed the public's insatiable appetite for the new medium by making a new full-length movie every few days, certainly would understand.

The Big Boss, shot in a remote village in Thailand, introduced what became the prototypical Lee action hero—the lone outsider, arriving or returning from Somewhere Else; a charismatic, self-contained man who is slow to anger but unstoppable when finally provoked.

Bruce is Cheng, an open-faced young man arriving at a Thai ice factory, where his Hong Kong relatives, good and simple folk, are among the expatriate workers. Early on, we find out that Cheng, apparently fleeing "trouble" in Hong Kong, has promised his mother never to resort to violence and Chinese boxing, or kung fu, again.

A fight sequence.

Shrewdly, the early fight scenes between the stalwart Hong Kong workers and the vicious thugs employed by the evil, drug-smuggling Big Boss, who likes "young chicks" and owns the ice factory, merely swirl around Bruce-as-Cheng, who, bound by his promise to stay out of trouble and never fight again, remains a bystander.

"Don't just stand there," one of the downtrodden workers exhorts him. "Fight!"

Cheng's upper lip quivers dangerously. Two precise, balletic kicks, and the knife-wielding attacker who has set upon him falls. The gang of amazed thugs flees in dismay. Says a drolly comedic second banana upon the arrival of

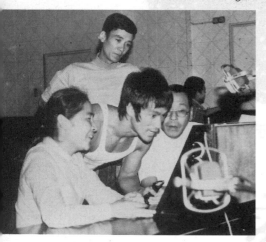

Chow Mei, the young girl (played by Maria Yi) who's been pining for Cheng: "We had some industrial unrest."

When Cheng does take on the entire gang, finally provoked by the abduction of Chow Mei and the massacre of his relatives, naturally he lays waste to all his enemies. Audiences had never seen anything like it: they cheered the unprecedented level of martial arts skill and precision in the battle scenes Lee himself had choreographed.

Boss broke box-office records in Hong Kong and all over Asia, in the process putting Golden Harvest on the film-world map. By December of 1971, Lee's star was rising in the East. Even a popular song of the day, "Lee Three Kicks," celebrated the new Asian cinematic hero.

While her husband was in Thailand shooting *Boss*, Linda Lee stayed in Los Angeles with her two children. The jump to the world of Asian film was such a leap into the unknown that the Lees had decided it was prudent not to leave the only home the children had ever known until the future was clearer. But even before *The Big Boss* was released it was making big waves.

The movie was being heralded by insiders, and expectation was so high that even before its midnight premiere (the late hour is a local tradition), Bruce came back to the United States to move his family to Hong Kong. "I had no inkling of what to expect when we got off the plane," Linda Lee recalls. "My first clue was that Bruce said on the plane that we needed to take a change of clothes before the plane landed so that we could look nice when we arrived at the airport, and I was sort of like, 'Why do we have to look nice when we arrive at the airport?'" But as soon as she saw the waiting crowds, she knew.

Her husband was famous.

With Bruce Lee's star already showing the unmistakable box-office signs of the unprecedented brightening to come, Raymond Chow signed him to a new contract—this time at twenty thousand dollars per picture.

A scene from *The Big Boss* where innocent young Cheng (Bruce) wakes up in bed with a girl in a "fancy house."

Because of Hong Kong's noise level, most films were shot without sound and dubbed later. This particular dubbing session was for Bruce's third film, *Return of the Dragon.*

Bruce and Linda celebrating Bruce's birthday with a cake depicting him kicking.

Bruce with Unicorn Chan (right).

CONNECTION

Not surprisingly, Bruce Lee's second movie was the one with which he felt the deepest personal connection.

Fist of Fury, known in the United States as *The Chinese Connection,* told a tale that would have had resonance for anyone who had grown up in Hong Kong, ceded to Britain a century and a half before as a prize of the colonial Opium Wars and occupied by Japanese invaders in World War II.

The picture also continued Lee's connection with many of his fellow *Big Boss* actors and crew members. Actresses Nora Miao and Maria Yi were in both films, both were written and directed by action director Lo Wei, and many of the villains in both were played by the same veteran Hong Kong character actors.

The film is set in Shanghai, China's great port city, in 1908, at a time when China, an ancient kingdom beset by internal strife and at the mercy of the outside great powers, was routinely referred to as the "sick man of Asia." Arrogant foreigners, particularly the Japanese and the British, swagger through Shanghai's streets. A sign at an embassy gate reads NO DOGS AND CHINESE ALLOWED.

Enter Bruce Lee as Chen Jeh, a returning martial arts student (from where, we never learn), who disembarks a ship just in time to learn that the beloved master of his "ching wu" school of Chinese boxing has died under mysterious circumstances. Soon, the supercilious spokesman for a rival Japanese karate school run by a criminal gang appears to announce the Chinese school's imminent takeover.

Contemptuous and imperious, the emissary calls the Chinese a "race of weaklings."

Bruce made many memorable appearances on Hong Kong television, such as on this 1971 telethon (to raise money for typhoon victims) during which young Brandon did his own demonstrations of board breaking.

Above: The house in Hong Kong at 41
Cumberland Road in Kowloon

Right: Bruce and family at the airport.

But the wicked masters of the karate dojo haven't reckoned with Chen. With his customary dramatic sense and visual acumen, Bruce Lee had choreographed for his character an awesome balletic confrontation with the entire assembled student body of the Japanese dojo. When Chen steps alone into their midst, the white gi-wearing karatemen quickly surround him, forming a lethal wheel, a slowly turning circle of attackers. In one of Lee's signature moves, Chen peels off his black coat and hurls it down; barechested and pumped, he fights back.

As they turn menacingly in one direction, he spins in the other, kicking, punching, and judo-throwing his way unharmed through the swirling onrush of their mass assault. Finally, producing a pair of nunchakus and striking at them from low to the practice floor, he demolishes his opponents, leaving them unconscious or writhing.

The battle between a Chinese hero and villains of other nationalities or ethnic groups, particularly Caucasians, was one convention of the Hong Kong action picture easy to label racist but perhaps more understandable given China's, and in particular Hong Kong's, long and bitter experience of colonial domination.

Later, the boss of the gang behind the dojo brings in Petrov, a mustachioed Russian (played by Bob Baker, an American martial artist), who can bend iron bars and drive nails through boards with bare closed hands.

In another innovation in the martial arts genre, Lee understood early the value of bringing in real martial artists as his movie opponents. Their skill allowed more complex choreography and added verisimilitude to the battle scenes. Martial artist Robert Wall, for example, made a convincing villain and went on to a larger movie career, as did another Lee film find, a karateist named Norris.

Bruce on a set .

When he meets Petrov in combat, Chen sets himself straddle-legged with a quick, businesslike tug at his pants leg (another Lee trademark move) for snapping side kicks from the horse position, then he overcomes the Russian with short, explosive shin-to-head kick combinations. And when the dojo's evil master attacks him with a samurai sword, Lee-as-Chen crisply kicks the sword out of the attacker's hand and into the air. As the sword tumbles in slow motion, Chen pulls his opponent's head down and forward: the blade plunges earthward and into the evil master's outstretched back!

In another telling scene a haughty and racist Japanese man, dressed in the traditional robes of feudal nobility, offers to accompany Chen Jeh past a bearded and turbaned guard who has blocked entry at a gate, but only if the young Chinese will get down on all fours. "Pretend you are a dog!" he demands contemptuously.

Chen responds to this outrage with sudden sharp blows that soundly defeat the arrogant Japanese and his companion. And with a single mighty kick, he destroys the racist no-dogs-or-Chinese sign forbidding passage. A crowd of watching peasants cheer this singular act of bravado and retaliation.

The Hong Kong Chinese in the movie audience, who knew something about humiliation and foreign occupation, cheered, too. They cheered the film's final image

as well: Chen caught in heroic freeze-frame as he leaps kicking at a line of pistol-wielding foreigners, his and his country's enemies, flying toward certain but honorable death.

For Bruce Lee, *The Chinese Connection* was an even bigger hit than his first film and one that broke his own box-office records all over the Asian theatrical circuit.

Within a single year of arriving back in Hong Kong and signing his original two-picture deal, Lee had gone supernova. His second contract, for twenty thousand per picture, was declared null and void, and the young star and Raymond Chow, the veteran producer, renegotiated their relationship, forming a production partnership.

Bruce with nunchakus.

Bruce Lee on the big screen could punch and kick better, and more convincingly, than anyone ever before. Now, after just two films, he also had the added kick of big-star clout.

And as anyone in Hollywood or in the world of Hong Kong filmmaking knows, when an actor is no longer tied by an exclusive contract *and* has clout, things happen. Lee, who knew that show-business power resides behind the camera rather than in front of it, formed his own production company, Concord, which coproduced his third film with Raymond Chow's Golden Harvest.

Bruce Lee not only starred in the picture but wrote and directed it as well. That level of overall responsibility was unprecedented for a Hong Kong movie actor, but Lee approached the daunting task of creating and overseeing his own motion picture in his usual methodical-student way, buying and reading a dozen or more books on the various behind-the-scenes filmmaking crafts and consulting collegially with the experienced "professors" on his crew.

The cordiality and respect he demonstrated then and on his other pictures toward the behind-the-scenes craftspeople (for example, he campaigned to raise the wages of Hong Kong's underpaid stuntpeople) earned him a lasting loyalty that show-business autocrats rarely see.

With this picture, Lee also earned the undying loyalty of the local Hong Kong audience by making it in the Cantonese dialect, which is spoken there. That may not seem unusual, but it was in fact the first Cantonese-language Hong Kong film since the late forties, when an influx of Shanghai filmmakers fleeing Mao Tse-tung and communism took over the Hong Kong film industry and began shooting pictures in their native Mandarin dialect, which

Maria Yi, Linda, Shannon, and Bruce at the airport

On the set with Linda, Shannon, and an unidentified man.

Bruce victoriously returning to Hong Kong after filming *Return of the Dragon* in Rome.

they then dubbed or subtitled in Cantonese. After Lee broke the barrier, Hong Kong filmmakers began making all their pictures in Cantonese again.

As early as his second picture, *The Chinese Connection,* an interlude where Lee's character assumes various disguises—as a rickshaw boy, an elderly newspaper vendor, and finally, as a bespectacled telephone lineman—suggested his dramatic range. Now, in *The Way of the Dragon* (known as *Return of the Dragon* in the United States), Lee wrote himself a role that showcased his comedic and light-romantic as well as his martial arts skills. Like his choice of opponents in his fight scenes, it was a shrewd move.

Of course, the writer-director-producer, who also has a credit as the "martial arts choreographer," scouted locations and cast the film as well, and for the climactic

confrontation he chose an American little known outside of martial-arts circles, a karate champion named Chuck Norris.

Lee was an admirer of the stylish and satirical "spaghetti Western" genre, pictures like *Fistful of Dollars* with characters like the Man With No Name, that had shot Clint Eastwood, one of Lee's show-business role models, to international stardom in the sixties. It's no coincidence that *Return* was filmed in Rome and that its soundtrack has that jaunty spaghetti Western feel. Though rarely remarked upon by film critics or by his legions of fans, this Lee-written and Lee-directed picture turns out to be a droll satire of the usually solemn, and sometimes pretentious, martial arts film itself.

Instead of the Man With No Name riding into the dusty town to save the small band of homesteaders from the evil bandits, we have Tang Lung, the handsome, young, and self-assured but decidedly unworldly martial artist flying into Rome to save the small band of honest Hong Kong restaurateurs—including the beautiful Nora Miao as the pouty-lipped, westernized Chen Ching Hua—who are being threatened by an Italian "syndicate" (i.e., the Mafia) that wants their establishment and its land.

Lee opens *Return of the Dragon* in the classic mode and with a telling shot that wordlessly, and wittily, sounds his favorite sociopolitical theme: an elderly, white-haired, hawk-profiled Caucasian woman, a strand of pearls around her neck, is peering myopically down her aquiline nose at the newly arrived stranger in town, a young man who is studiously trying to ignore her rude stare. They're in the bustling Rome airport, and when at last she leaves, Tang, the stranger from the Hong Kong hinterland, sighs with relief.

Lee-as-Tang is the pack-toting innocent abroad, the country boy in the big city. "I'm here to get you out of this mess," he says confidently (in a deep, dubbed voice), when

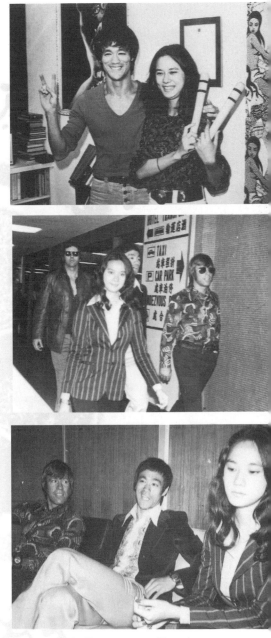

Bruce and his *Return* costars Nora Miao and Chuck Norris.

pretty Chen Ching picks him up in her white Oldsmobile convertible. Tang takes one look at her big land boat and exclaims: "BMW? Mustang? . . . It's a Rolls!"

When she takes him to see impressive ancient Roman ruins, Tang sizes them up immediately, saying, "Our slums are just like this."

Lee's direction is brisk and muscular; his Tang is polite, shy, jokey, and jaunty—a character who draws on both Lee's own personality and experiences as a stranger in a foreign land.

At an outdoor café in a colorful piazza, Chen Ching explains the local customs, saying that when people smile at you in Rome you smile back, while behind her at a nearby table, a flirtatious Sophia Loren look-alike, with sloe eyes, big bones, and even bigger hair, is giving Tang a smoldering come-hither look. What's a polite young fellow from Hong Kong to do? With a when-in-Rome shrug, Tang smiles back, and in a flash (and much to Chen Ching's chagrin) the Italian woman has moved in on him, fairly purring in his ear.

Later, when the thugs first appear at the restaurant, they have an early seventies "mod" look about them— with their tie-dyes, colorful silks, and hip-hugging bell-bottoms—that even then must have looked farcical and ironic. The head henchman, in the employ of the white-haired Caucasian who is the syndicate leader, is a fey and mincing Asian, who at one point pats Tang's chest and admires his "rippling muscles."

At first, when the thugs disrupt the restaurant, the earnest employees try to fight back using karate, a "foreign" martial art. When that's to no avail, it's Tang's turn, but first he's only too happy to provide a lesson in Chinese boxing. "Put your hip into it," he explains, in a line that would make any martial arts student smile: it's how you get "some" power.

"Dragon seeks path," says Tang tartly, punching and kicking through the thugs in the alley behind the restau-

rant. "Dragon whips his tail." He beats them one by one or as they attack in groups.

The kung fu moves are realistic, and the choreography is, as usual, brilliant and thrilling, but when Lee ends his devastating counterattacks with a Three Stooges–like fillip, a tiny poke, or perhaps a dismissive backhand thwap under the chin, his satirical intentions are clear.

"It was all Bruce," says Linda Lee of the film she calls her favorite Bruce Lee picture. "The clowning around . . . it was the way he acted at home."

The syndicate boss, his thugs in disarray and his power in question, has no choice: he sends for the dreaded Colt (Norris), the martial artist he calls "America's best."

Their final confrontation unfolds to the accompaniment of ominous spaghetti Western–like theme music within the rough-stone vaults of Rome's ancient Colosseum, where gladiators once fought to the death. The panoramic establishing shot—when the two antagonists first meet—was filmed at the actual famous outdoor amphitheater, with footage of Norris in his white gi high in the stands, saluting Lee with an imperial thumbs-down, and of Lee, his legs and arms pumping like pistons, running up the steeply sloped stone stairs to meet the enemy. However, the actual battle was shot on a stage in Hong Kong in front of a Colosseum photo backdrop.

It's not a simple fight; as staged by Lee, it's as dramatic a confrontation between good and evil as any Eastwood shoot-out on the high plains.

Not a word is exchanged. Colt loosens up with knuckle cracks and shoulder rolls; the men fire off a flurry of shadowboxing punches and kicks.

Director Lee cuts away to quick tight shots of scrawny, hyperalert kittens—the city and particularly the Colosseum were well known for the immense population of feral cats—seeming ready to strike. The cats . . . the men . . .

A big-eyed kitty in gigantic close-up screeches.

The men begin to fight.

Bruce doing one of his many stretching exercises. Bruce tended to stretch throughout the day using these movements to continuously tone his body.

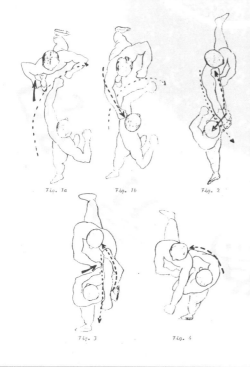

Hairy, fleshy Colt versus smooth and wiry Tang. The detailed choreography Lee worked out covered twenty pages. At first, Colt seems unstoppable. Down goes Tang.

On his back and in trouble, Tang reaches up, grabs a fistful of his opponent's abundant chest hair . . . and rips it out. Leaping up, he slowly opens his closed fist and, raising it in front of his face, blows the unseen hair away.

The moment recalls upstart Lee's real-life past battles over his attitude toward classic technique: the "right" technique, he used to say, infuriating his karate critics, is the one that works. Colt's no-no finger-waggle warning, after the sudden chest-hair counter turns the course of the fight, becomes the punchline for director Lee's droll little visual joke.

Tang briskly brushes himself off and begins a bouncy little boxer's dance. The battle resumes.

It continues in slow motion, with no cuts for editing or camera moves, Tang dodging and parrying Colt's unrelenting attack, then counterattacking with low kicks to the knees and shins, inside blocks, and rapid-fire punches. A low leg sweep leaves Colt twitching and hobbling, but, though both men know the inevitable result, the indomitable warrior attacks one last time. Tang snaps Colt's neck. In a gesture of respect for his fallen opponent Tang covers Colt's face with the gi.

The little band of honest homesteaders rescued, his duty done, the stoic stranger departs. In the farewell scene at a picturesque Rome cemetery, Chen Ching looks appropriately stricken. One of the restaurant workers, heretofore merely a comic-relief second banana, watches wistfully as Tang, their savior, leaves. "In this world of guns and knives, wherever (he) may go," the second banana declaims mournfully, "he will travel alone."

The Man With No Name never had a better leave-taking. Once again Bruce Lee broke his own box-office records in Hong Kong, and Asian movie magazines devoted entire issues to Lee and his new film.

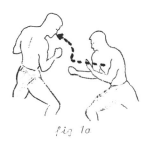 

fig 1a	fig 1b	fig 1c
low feint to body	flow with timing to hook	ends with left cross

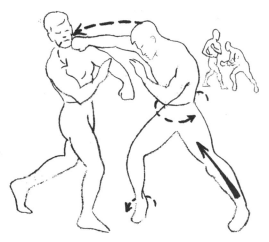

low feint to body follow with
right hook (same hand---one continuous movement)

The Left Cross---after
drawing opponent's right

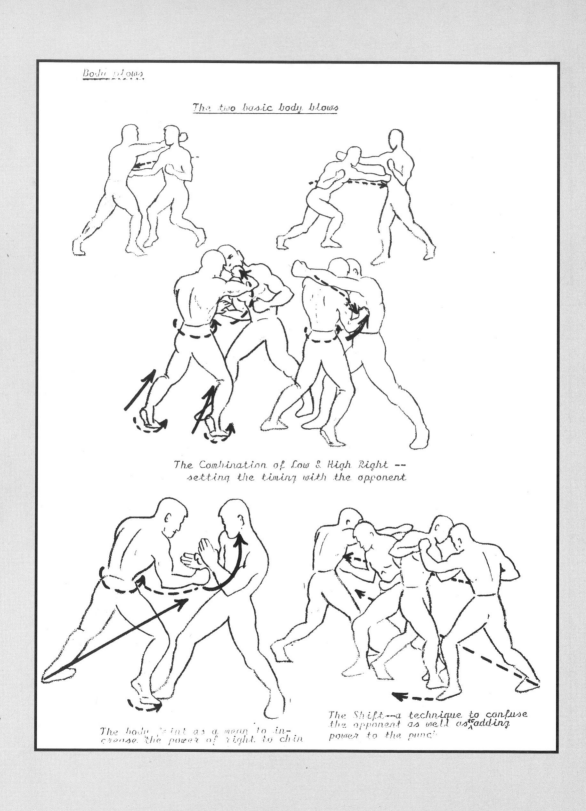

The two basic body blows

The Combination of Low & High Right —
setting the timing with the opponent

The body feint as a mean to in-
crease the power of right to chin

The Shift—a technique to confuse
the opponent as well as adding
power to the punch

always keep the left hand guard up! Be ready to follow with left.

Unlike the straight punch, the striking hand shoulder should raise high, this gives extra leverage and protects your own jaw while punching.

according to the position of yourself and your man and the time you have to put the punch in, you may occasionally take a short step to the left, just a few inches, with your left foot (watch out for kicks). This will put even more weight into the punch, especially at fairly long range, and take you out of danger of a reply from the opponent's hands.

The upward hook--you screw the blow in and up so that you can send it to chin of a man with his face covered up by his arm held across it. On the other hand, the horizontal hook and the forward hook will go "over" that kind of guard.

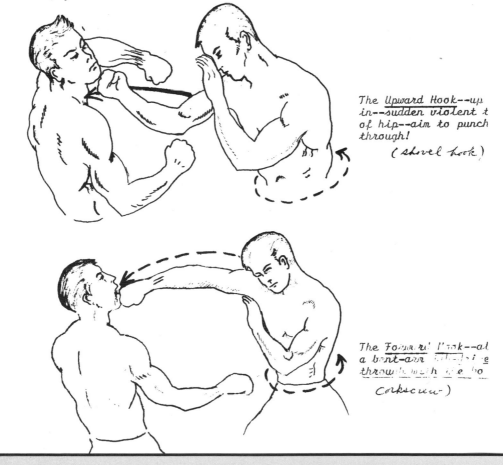

The Upward Hook--up in--sudden violent t of hip--aim to punch through!
(shovel hook)

The Forward hook--al a bent-arm   g throuh with e ho
(corkscrew)

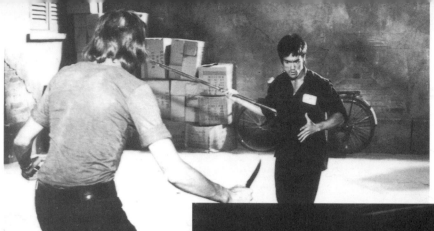

Various scenes of Bruce with actor Chuck Norris. Bruce gave him his start in film, and Norris went on to become a superstar in his own right.

Bruce not only wrote, directed, and produced *Return of the Dragon*— he starred in it as well. He also cast and choreographed the film. Here he is screen-testing a young actress and rehearsing a scene.

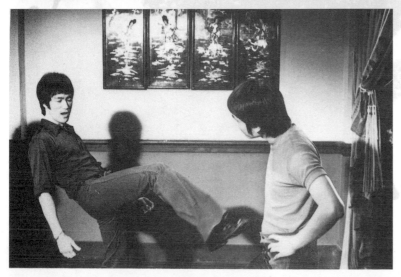

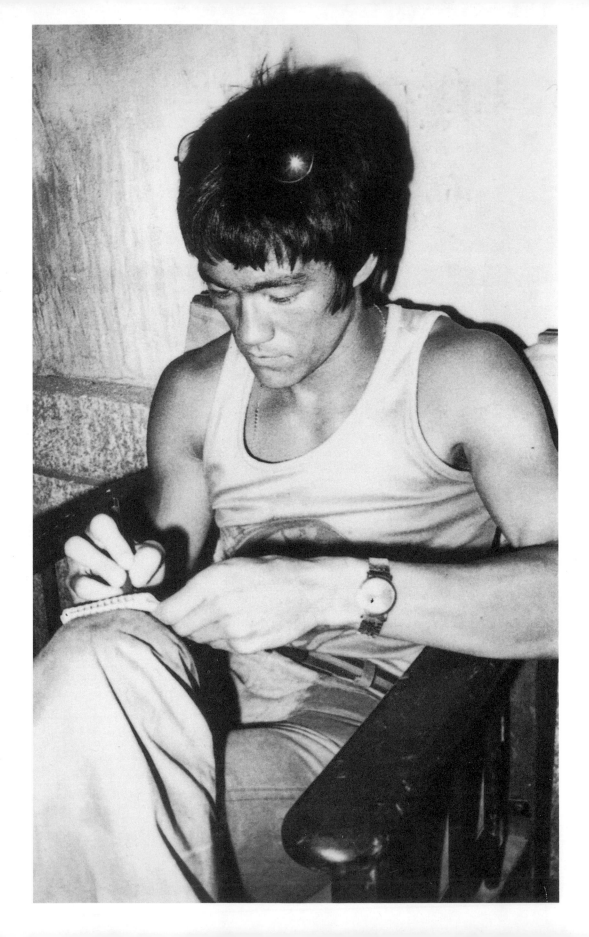

Bruce with Raymond Chow in 1972.

G-BB

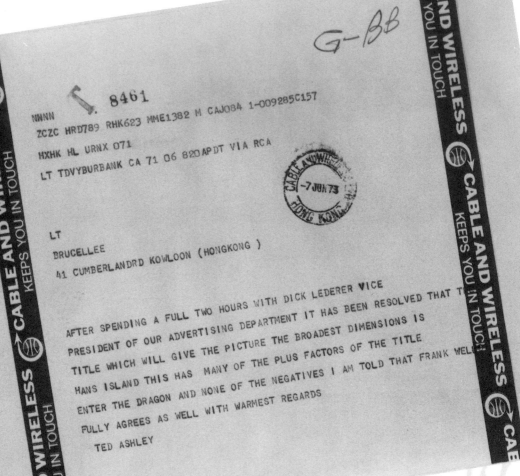

NNNN 🖐 8461

ZCZC HRD789 RHK623 MME1382 M CAJO84 1-009285C157

HXHK HL URNX 071

LT TDVYBURBANK CA 71 06 820APDT VIA RCA

-7 JUN 73

LT

BRUCELLEE

41 CUMBERLANDRD KOWLOON (HONGKONG)

AFTER SPENDING A FULL TWO HOURS WITH DICK LEDERER VICE
PRESIDENT OF OUR ADVERTISING DEPARTMENT IT HAS BEEN RESOLVED THAT T
TITLE WHICH WILL GIVE THE PICTURE THE BROADEST DIMENSIONS IS
HANS ISLAND THIS HAS MANY OF THE PLUS FACTORS OF THE TITLE
ENTER THE DRAGON AND NONE OF THE NEGATIVES I AM TOLD THAT FRANK WELL
FULLY AGREES AS WELL WITH WARMEST REGARDS

TED ASHLEY

HAN'S ISLAND

Even though Bruce Lee had become an internationally known action film star merely by making a couple of films for the Asian action market, he wasn't a Hollywood star, which to Tinseltown was all that mattered. But the industry that had dismissed him after *The Green Hornet* couldn't dismiss him after his pictures started outgrossing films like *The Sound of Music* and *The Godfather* in the Far East, and a big Hollywood studio now joined Lee's own production company to make a film that would be the biggest and best martial arts picture ever seen.

The production would be headed by Fred Weintraub, the producer who also was involved in the original development of the *Kung Fu* TV series, and Robert Clouse, the director who, with Weintraub, went on to do the China O'Brien pictures, starring Cynthia Rothrock, in the early 1990s.

It would have a big budget, thirteen weeks of Hong Kong location shooting, "name" actors, and a James Bond flair. But what to call it?

"There was big controversy about the naming," recalls Linda Lee. "There were telegrams that *flew* back and forth across the Pacific about the naming of this movie."

Lee favored the title he had originally chosen for his own directing debut, *Enter the Dragon,* but a Hollywood studio executive had another idea. He telegrammed a brusquely worded fiat to the studio's newest star: the wiser heads of Hollywood had decided that the title *Enter the Dragon* wouldn't play as well as *Han's Island.*

"Bruce was insisting that it be called *Enter the Dragon,*" Linda Lee continues. "He felt so strongly about that, and they said [at the studio], 'Oh, it's too Chinese; it

Bruce and Han, the archvillain of *Enter the Dragon*, battling.

doesn't describe anything; people won't know that your [nick]name is the Little Dragon,' and on and on." So *Han's Island* would be the title. Period.

It wasn't that it was a bad title. After all, Han (played memorably by Chinese actor Shih Kien, who at the time spoke no English and knew his dialogue by rote) is the villain of the piece, a renegade Shaolin monk, master of a private army and a palatial island fortress, who smuggles drugs and forcibly addicts pretty young women to them so he can sell them into prostitution—in short, the very incarnation of the dark side of The Force.

Once every three years, we are informed in a before-the-opening-credits prologue set in an idyllic Shaolin temple, Han holds a world-class martial arts tournament on his island. To infiltrate the island and prove the case against Han, Braithwaite, a British spymaster, comes to the temple to recruit "Mister Lee."

At first, Lee is a most reluctant secret agent. Clearly, he'd prefer to stay in his temple paradise, demonstrating Thai boxing in front of the approving orange- and yellow-robed monks and teaching young students the fundamentals of his arcane art.

Pointing skyward with his index finger, he memorably tells one sullen young man, in dialogue that Lee himself added to the script, "Don't think, *feel*. It is like a finger pointing a way to the moon. Don't concentrate on the finger or you will miss all that heavenly glory."

But agree to go he does, and in flashback we see why—just as in flashback we learn why two Americans, Williams (Jim Kelly, an American karate tournament champion) and Roper (John Saxon, an actor who himself was a longtime student of the martial arts), also have arrived.

Williams is on the run after defending himself against racist cops, while Roper, an inveterate gambler, is fleeing debts to a loan shark. But Lee isn't just undercover; he has a personal reason to come.

Lee's courageous sister, Su Lin (Angela Mao Ying), pur-

sued and finally trapped by Han's henchmen, has killed herself with a shard of broken glass rather than submitting to Han's cruel chief bodyguard Oharra (Robert Wall).

On his island, Han lives like a feudal despot—complete with medieval banquet—which is to say like the archvillain in a James Bond film. "Very few people can be totally ruthless," he says, and he has no qualms about ordering men to fight and to die. Whispers Mei Ling (Betty Chung), the pretty agent Braithwaite had earlier placed in Han's employ, "People disappear."

"We forge our bodies in the fire of our will," declares Han, who is disconcertingly apt to replace his missing hand with steel talons and other lethal prosthetics, so Lee must fight. But not before he gives a bullying thug a demonstration of his style.

On the junk going to the island, the thug had been carelessly pushing the Asian crew around. When the thug scowlingly demands to know Lee's fighting style, Lee replies mildly, "You can call it the art of fighting without fighting," and he tricks the thug into a small boat, which, to the crew's delight, Lee casts off to founder in the junk's wake.

In an unscripted moment the thug is last seen scrambling about in the nearly swamped skiff. In reality, rough seas on the day of shooting nearly sent the real actor over the side.

Hundreds of extras and a Hollywood-size crew were assembled for this movie, and the 1972 shoot abounded with stories of minor and near mishaps: a bite from a defanged snake that could have seriously sidelined the star, a cut on a "prop bottle" that turned out to be made of real glass and did force Lee to stop shooting for nearly a week, and challenges by unknown local actors in the cast looking to make their reputations by defeating and dethroning the new Hong Kong king.

Of course, with a Hollywood studio involved it's hard to know how many of these gunslinging invitations to

Battling continues as the dragon returns.

Bruce pictured with martial arts champion Jim Kelly.

fight were real and how many staged for the benefit of a gullible press. Not that Lee, like his character "Lee," didn't have to do his share of outwitting, and perhaps even outpunching, bullying thugs determined to test his style in real-life single combat, but it's hard to imagine the picture's veteran Hollywood producer and its veteran Hollywood action director, both of whom were nearly always on location, allowing anyone with bad intentions anywhere near their studio's marquee-value star.

When "Lee" finally faces the cruel Oharra in the tournament in single combat, he demonstrates a more lethal aspect of his style. As in *Return,* Bruce Lee used the opportunity to incorporate another reference to his past real-world martial disputes. To intimidate him before the combat, Oharra breaks a board with one fierce hit. Says "Lee," the character in the film, in a line lifted from the public comments of Lee the martial artist and the man, "Boards don't hit back."

Forearms raised and open backhands lightly touching, poised like two fencers crossing blades, Oharra and Lee wait for the starter's signal. But each time the word is given, before Oharra can even twitch a muscle to strike, Lee, with his superior reflexes, smashes into him with a single, lightning-fast blow.

With a vision in his mind of his tormented sister holding the glass shard toward her own belly, Lee destroys Oharra with his fists, with a spinning reverse crescent kick, and with a pile-driver side kick. When the defeated Oharra picks up a broken bottle, Lee leaps upon the fallen bodyguard, flying into the air in slow motion and landing on him with both feet. As he twists downward onto Oharra, Lee has a look on his face mixing anguish with the terrifying grimace of the wild-eyed warrior.

But more deadly confrontations are still to come. In the underground cavern below Han's palace, Lee fights off an army of attackers, beating at them with a long staff he later breaks into two sticks and with the inevitable

nunchakus. Finally, with Han's pris-
oners freed and his private army in
disarray, Lee stalks the criminal
warlord himself in his private mu-
seum and in a mirrored maze.

"You have offended my family
and you have offended a Shaolin
temple," Lee says, as if pronouncing
a death sentence. Han throws a
spear that narrowly misses him.

In the battle, Lee spear-hands
Han, catches him with a back-
spinning reverse crescent kick, and,
pulling Han down into a headlock,
back-kicks him in the face. When
Han rakes him with his metal talons,
Lee, in a now familiar gesture, tastes
his own blood, then side-kicks to
Han's face, finally kicking him back
into the point of his own spear.

With *Enter the Dragon* director Robert
Clouse.

Another Bruce Lee film victory,
and in real life the film was a tri-
umph, too. The studio executives backed down, acced-
ing to their star's wish in naming the film, which went on
to gross more than one hundred million dollars at the box
office, an unparalleled feat for a Hong Kong martial
arts film.

On July 20, 1973, plans were well under way for a trip
back to the United States for the picture's Los Angeles premiere and a publicity tour. Linda Lee was waiting at home
when the phone rang. At first she thought it was some
kind of joke, but she took a taxi to the hospital anyway.

Though he surely must have sensed a new level of
renown was coming, Bruce Lee—young, strong, and
showbiz savvy—didn't live to see the triumphant box-
office progress of *Enter the Dragon.*

Many of the tournament scenes in *Enter the Dragon* were shot within the walled tennis courts of an estate belonging to Bruce's lawyer. When an extra challenged Bruce to prove his fighting skills, scores of other actors would watch. (Their legs and feet are shown dangling in the upper right of this photograph.) It seemed there was always a camera there to shoot these confrontations, news of which often made the Hong Kong papers as well.

Above: Director Raymond Clouse about to cut his birthday cake with a sword from the set. From the marks on Bruce's chest and cheek you can tell which scenes they are in the process of filming.

Opposite: Bruce and actor John Saxon interacting. In the lower photograph producer Raymond Chow looks on.

武林人士必讀的武術雜誌

當代武壇

14
HK$1.50

MARTIAL
MAGAZINE

本刊武術專欄作家黃不名
※突接恐嚇信！
香港選手購備「夕
※第三屆東南亞□□□□講賽
四屆拳擊冠軍□
※劉大川衛冕失敗的內在因素
※亞太地區第一屆空手道大賽

Bruce is on the ground here, battling one of the hundred extras that Hollywood employed for the film *Enter the Dragon*.

李小龍

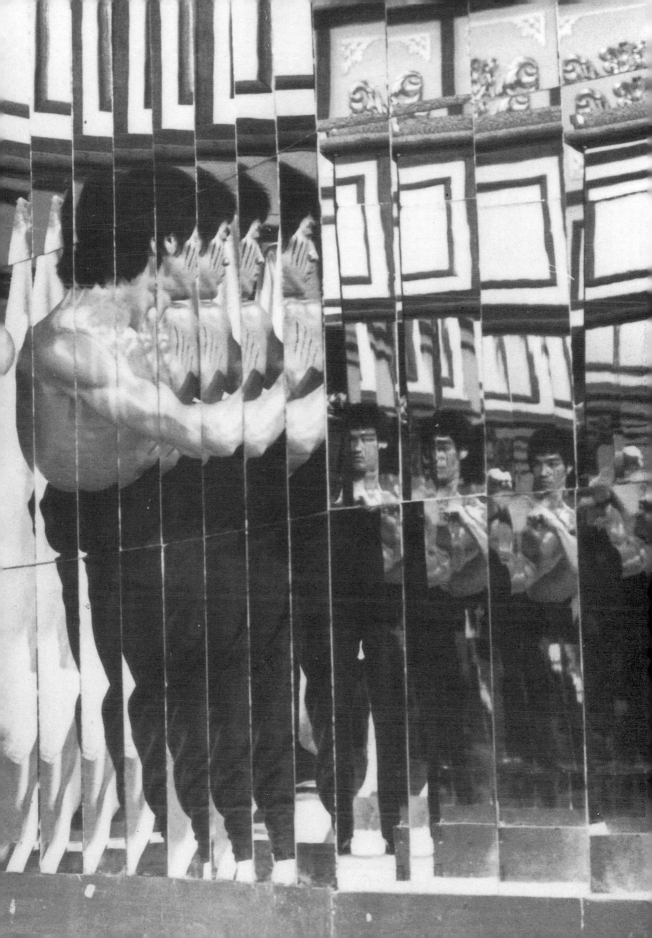

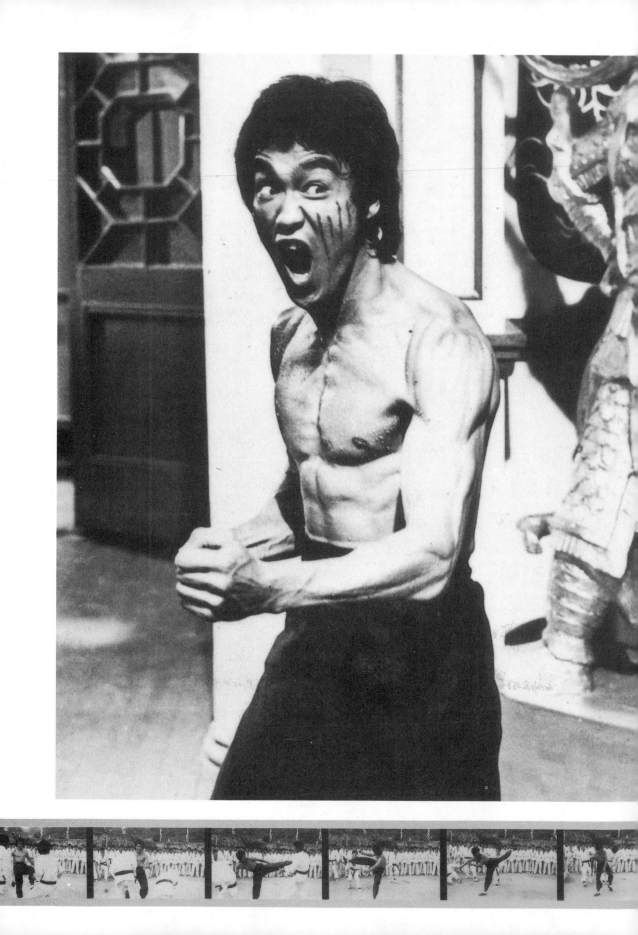

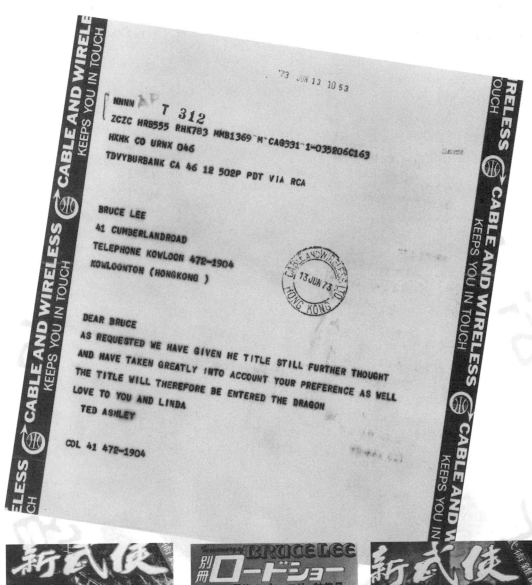

```
                                                    '73 JUN 13 10 53

  NNNN  AP T 312
  ZCZC HRB555 RHK783 MMB1369 ~M~CA8331~1-035206C163
  HXHK CO URNX 046
  TDVYBURBANK CA 46 12 502P PDT VIA RCA


  BRUCE LEE
  41 CUMBERLANDROAD
  TELEPHONE KOWLOON 472-1904
  KOWLOONTON (HONGKONG)


  DEAR BRUCE
  AS REQUESTED WE HAVE GIVEN HE TITLE STILL FURTHER THOUGHT
  AND HAVE TAKEN GREATLY INTO ACCOUNT YOUR PREFERENCE AS WELL
  THE TITLE WILL THEREFORE BE ENTERED THE DRAGON
  LOVE TO YOU AND LINDA
      TED ASHLEY


  COL 41 472-1904
```

The
GAME

Dead at thirty-two of a cerebral edema, or swelling, brought on by an allergic reaction to ingredients in a prescription headache tablet. So said the Hong Kong coroner. Chaotic crowds of tens of thousands of mourners jammed the narrow Hong Kong streets outside his funeral. But nearly five years after Bruce Lee's shockingly sudden death, an American studio released a "new" Bruce Lee film.

Ironically, in *Game of Death* there were more known American actors—Gig Young, Dean Jagger, and Hugh O'Brian—than in any of Bruce Lee's previous films, but they were just window dressing for a preposterous and exploitative plot, and none of them had an actual scene with the star. In fact, their scenes were filmed years later and combined with footage Lee had shot before for a far different project.

If *Return of the Dragon* was Lee's homage to the Western and *Enter the Dragon* was his James Bond, then *Game of Death,* as he originally conceived it, was to be his philosophical martial arts epic. It began production as his fourth film.

Game would be a classic quest picture, set in a mysterious, multileveled pagoda, with each level guarded by the master of a particular fighting style. Lee's character would have to fight his way from level to level, past opponent after opponent.

In the ad hoc world of Hong Kong filmmaking it was far from unusual for a "hot" actor or director to work on more than one picture at a time, and the guerrilla-band nature of the process made it relatively easy to take advantage of a fortuitous circumstance—such as the visit to the Crown Colony by Kareem Abdul-Jabbar.

Bruce with Dan Inosanto and nunchakus. Inosanto, Bruce's senior student in the practice of jeet kune do, was actually the one who introduced him to the nunchakus.

The seven-foot-two Los Angeles Lakers basketball star was one of Bruce Lee's most famous, and most unlikely, students. The basketball player had been studying with Lee since the mid-sixties, when he was known as Lew Alcindor and was playing college ball.

The *Game* shoot "came about in a hurry," Linda Lee recalls, "because Kareem Jabbar, who was his friend and student for a long time, was coming to visit Hong Kong, and Danny Inosanto [who was Lee's student of longest standing] was coming to visit, and so he kind of put together this plot that he'd wanted to use these people [in] because they're so good to fight against."

The men were perfect for roles as two of the opposing martial arts masters, and just as he was finishing *Return of the Dragon,* Bruce Lee filmed *Game* fight scenes with them, as well as shots of his character, in a formfitting yellow bodysuit with black stripes, of the type motorcycle racers wear, running up a wooden stairway. Those fights end the picture titled *Game of Death.*

With that footage done, Lee turned his attention to his Hollywood studio coproduction, intending to finish *Game* when *Enter the Dragon* was completed.

By then Lee's stardom was incandescent. Much on his mind in this period of whirlwind activity were both the craft of acting and the craft of living. Just months before his demise, he wrote what amounted to a testament: "I am still in my own process of learning, constantly discovering and constantly growing. If this assignment is not tough enough, I am in the midst of preparing my next movie, *Enter the Dragon,* a coproduction between Concord and Warner Bros., plus another Concord production, *The [sic] Game of Death,* which is only halfway done. . . ."

He concluded his handwritten remarks with what now reads as a valedictory, a message to those with whom he'd battled both metaphorically and literally over the years, his fellow martial artists: "I hope my fellow martial artist[s] would open up and be transparently real and I wish them well in their own process of finding their own cause."

Years after their star's death, the *Game* producers used stunt doubles and footage from Lee's previous movies to create a "plot" that played on the audience's knowledge of that untimely death and of the swirl of speculation surrounding it—the same kind of conspiratorial theorizing, impossible to satisfactorily answer, that arose after the sudden deaths of both Marilyn and Elvis.

Game, as released, is the story of martial arts star Billy Lo (ostensibly Lee but mostly played by a double) who, because he will not cooperate with criminals, is shot in the face with a real bullet surreptitiously placed in a stunt gun. (Years later, of course, in a case of life tragically imitating bad art, Brandon Lee died on a film set, in an accident involving a misloaded gun.)

The scene Billy is filming is a re-creation of the final shot from *The Chinese Connection,* when Lee-as-Chen, unarmed, charges a line of foreigners armed with guns.

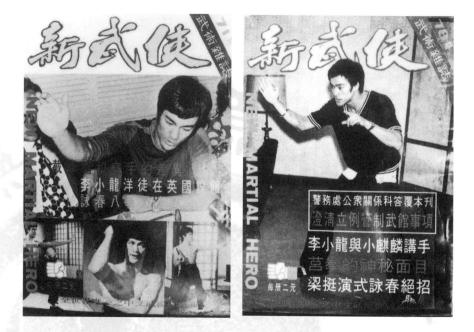

In *Game,* footage from both that movie and the final confrontation with Chuck Norris in *Return of the Dragon* is intercut with not very convincing shots of the double.

BILLY LO DIES, scream newspaper headlines, but secretly he's been taken for reconstructive surgery that has "permanently altered" his face.

This expedient plot device may explain why the double, who has the same general body type as Lee, doesn't really look like Bruce Lee at all. It adds a bandaged face to the sorry gallery of tricks the movie uses to hide the double's own features.

At various times, the double wears big tinted sunglasses or a thick towel wrapped around his neck, sports a fake beard or a motorcycle helmet, and is shot at a distance in profile or in shadows. But when it comes to the fighting, it's particularly easy to see that this graceless brawler is not Bruce Lee.

The footage shot "after he died had *nothing* to do with what Bruce was doing," says Linda Lee emphatically.

Nothing can redeem the ludicrousness that has come before, but at least the movie's final confrontations are the real thing: Bruce Lee and Danny Inosanto dueling with nunchakus (Inosanto, in fact, had first introduced Lee to the weapon) and Lee shooting leaping head kicks at the gigantic Abdul-Jabbar.

Finally, *Game*'s end credits unreel over a montage of moments from Lee's three previous Golden Harvest pictures.

To see these images is to wonder what might have been. "I think Bruce probably would have been very successful after *Enter the Dragon* and done many more films in the United States," says Linda Lee. Finally, Hollywood would have been open to him, and he would have moved behind the camera, directing and producing. "He eventually would have steered away from martial arts totally. His goal with martial arts was to show the beauty of the Chinese culture. . . . He wanted to integrate it more into showing it as a way of life, rather than just beating people up."

In a last irony *The Silent Flute,* which could have been Lee's first breakthrough film in the early seventies, actually was produced at the end of that decade. Retitled *Circle of Iron,* it starred . . . David Carradine.

Bruce Lee's ultimate impact, though, far exceeded anything that could be measured at the box office. In his brief career he had shattered long-held stereotypes and broken strong social barriers, in a sense fulfilling the early fervent hope best symbolized by his own Chinese birth name: Jun Fan.

The literal meaning of "Jun," a common Chinese boy's name in Hong Kong, is "to arouse to the active state or to make prosperous." The name implied a wish, well understood by the Hong Kong Chinese of Bruce Lee's father's generation, for the restoration of prosperity to their long-

David and Goliath: Bruce and former Los Angeles Lakers star Kareem Abdul-Jabbar.

suffering nation. "Fan" comes partly from "San Fan Si," the Chinese name for the city of San Francisco, where Bruce was born. "Fan," too, has more than one meaning and would have been understood by the Chinese of the time as suggesting both a garden and a subordinate country bordering a big, powerful country. Thus, the full meaning of "Jun Fan" reflected a father's hope that his son would grow shining and prosperous on foreign land and that some day he would rise to disturb the foreigners' complacent sense of superiority. In a larger sense, perhaps, Jun Fan might even usher in the return of an era of respect for his own people.

Game of Death went on to gross one hundred million dollars worldwide, according to one report. The reputation of a lesser talent might have suffered from such a misbegotten exploitation, but not Bruce Lee's—perhaps because it wasn't simply his educated hands and feet that had taken him so far so fast. His brief, meteoric rise was a product of an unusually disciplined and wide-ranging mind. He well understood the game he was in, too—"a strange marriage of art and business," he'd called it—and its irresistible imperative: take the money and *run*!

But even in death, as in life,
he rose above such crass considerations
with a simple but profound philosophy:
Walk on.

Linda Lee consoled by Raymond Chow as she leaves the hospital where Bruce has just died.